The Scarecrow Author Bibliographies

1. John Steinbeck (Tetsumaro Hayashi). 1973.
2. Joseph Conrad (Theodore G. Ehrsam). 1969.
3. Arthur Miller (Tetsumaro Hayashi). 2d ed. 1976.
4. Katherine Anne Porter (Waldrip & Bauer). 1969.
5. Philip Freneau (Philip M. Marsh). 1970.
6. Robert Greene (Tetsumaro Hayashi). 1971.
7. Benjamin Disraeli (R. W. Stewart). 1972.
8. John Berryman (Richard W. Kelly). 1972.
9. William Dean Howells (Vito J. Brenni). 1973.
10. Jean Anouilh (Kathleen W. Kelly). 1973.
11. E. M. Forster (Alfred Borrello). 1973.
12. The Marquis de Sade (E. Pierre Chanover). 1973.
13. Alain Robbe-Grillet (Dale W. Frazier). 1973.
14. Northrop Frye (Robert D. Denham). 1974.
15. Federico García Lorca (Laurenti & Siracusa). 1974.
16. Ben Jonson (Brock & Welsh). 1974.
17. Four French Dramatists: Eugène Brieux, François de Curel, Emile Fabre, Paul Hervieu (Edmund F. Santa Vicca). 1974.
18. Ralph Waldo Ellison (Jacqueline Covo). 1974.
19. Philip Roth (Bernard F. Rodgers, Jr.). 1974.
20. Norman Mailer (Laura Adams). 1974.
21. Sir John Betjeman (Margaret Stapleton). 1974.
22. Elie Wiesel (Molly Abramowitz). 1974.
23. Paul Laurence Dunbar (Eugene W. Metcalf, Jr.). 1975.
24. Henry James (Beatrice Ricks). 1975.
25. Robert Frost (Lentricchia & Lentricchia). 1976.
26. Sherwood Anderson (Douglas G. Rogers). 1976.
27. Iris Murdoch and Muriel Spark (Tominaga & Schneidermeyer). 1976.
28. John Ruskin (Kirk H. Beetz). 1976.
29. Georges Simenon (Trudee Young). 1976.
30. George Gordon, Lord Byron (Oscar José Santucho). 1976.
31. John Barth (Richard Vine). 1977.
32. John Hawkes (Carol A. Hryciw). 1977.
33. William Everson (Bartlett & Campo). 1977.
34. May Sarton (Lenora Blouin). 1978.
35. Wilkie Collins (Kirk H. Beetz). 1978.
36. Sylvia Plath (Lane & Stevens). 1978.
37. E. B. White (A. J. Anderson). 1978.
38. Henry Miller (Lawrence J. Shifreen). 1978.

E. B. WHITE
A Bibliography

by

A.J. Anderson

The Scarecrow Author Bibliographies, No. 37

The Scarecrow Press, Inc.
Metuchen, N.J. & London
1978

Library of Congress Cataloging in Publication Data

Anderson, Arthur James.
E.B. White--a bibliography.

(The Scarecrow author bibliographies ; no. 37)
Includes index.
1. White, Elwyn Brooks, 1899- --Bibliography. I. Title.
Z8970.36.A52 [PS3545.H5187] 016.818'5'209
ISBN 0-8108-1121-9 78-2783

Manufactured in the United States of America

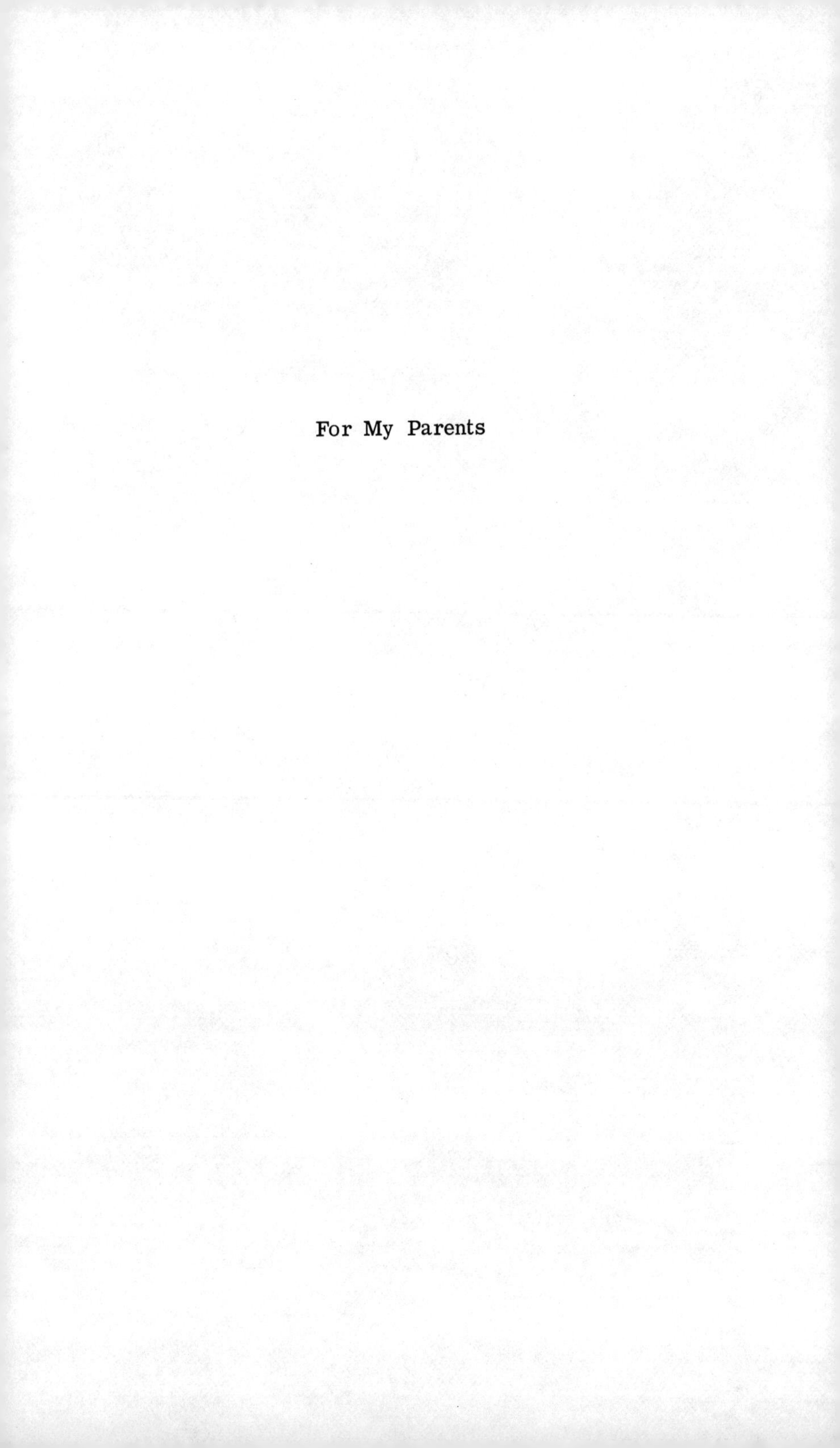

For My Parents

CONTENTS

Introduction 1

Part I. WRITINGS BY E. B. WHITE

Books and Pamphlets 5

Verse 8

Articles, Short Stories, and Other Prose Pieces 26

Editorials 124

Reviews
- Theatre 133
- Cinema 135
- Books 136

Forewords, Introductions, and Contributions to the Works of Others 138

Miscellaneous
- Personal Column, Seattle Daily Times 139
- Answers to Hard Questions, The New Yorker 140
- These Precious Days, The New Yorker 142
- Obituaries, The New Yorker 142
- Other 143

Part II. WRITINGS ABOUT E. B. WHITE

Biography and Criticism 147

Reviews of E. B. White's Books 151

INDEX (Authors and Titles) 165

INTRODUCTION

E. B. White occupies a unique position among contemporary writers--children and adults read him. Children know him as the author of Stuart Little, Charlotte's Web, and The Trumpet of the Swan; his name suggests charming tales and good fun. Adults know him as a contributor to The New Yorker and Harper's Magazine and coauthor, with William Strunk, Jr., of The Elements of Style; to them his name suggests polished wit, a civilized attitude, a masterly prose style, and a defender of the right of privacy. He has been described variously as "one of the country's most precious, literary resources," "the most influential of living American prose writers," "our best living personal essayist." His honors and awards have been many: honorary degrees from Dartmouth, Yale, Harvard, the gold medal of the National Institute of Arts and Letters, the Laura Ingalls Wilder Award, the National Medal for Literature, the Presidential Medal of Freedom, to name a few.

Elwyn Brooks White was born in Mount Vernon, New York, in 1899. He attended public school there, writing short stories, poems, and editorials for his high school newspaper, before going to Cornell University, where he earned an A.B. degree in 1921. He became a member of the staff of the Cornell Daily Sun in his freshman year, and served as the paper's editor-in-chief in his senior year. After five years of travel and a variety of jobs, during which time he contributed poems and other pieces to F. P. A.'s column "The Conning Tower" and Christopher Morley's column "The Bowling Green" and stinted as a reporter and columnist for the Seattle Times, he joined the staff of the fledgling New Yorker in 1926. His name became practically synonymous with The New Yorker; over the years he has written the "Notes and Comment" column (the opening essay in the magazine), edited and contributed to the "Talk of the Town" section, devised captions and taglines for newsbreak fillers, and produced numerous other items of prose and verse. (He still edits the newsbreaks, and writes their taglines or headings, for the bottoms of New Yorker columns.) From October 1938 until May 1943 he conducted the "One Man's Meat" department in Harper's Magazine. Many of his poems and prose pieces have been collected in book form.

The purpose of this bibliography is to provide access to White's writings for scholars and students; thus, it does not include the elaborate descriptive characteristics of a formal bibliography. In the "Books and Pamphlets" section of Part I, only original publications and new editions (or where new introductions and/or revised chapters have been added) are listed; reprints are not given. Although many of White's books, particularly his children's books, have been translated into several foreign languages, the bibliography covers only English-language publications. (White has donated many of his original manuscripts to Cornell; the library also has copies of his books in foreign languages.) The bibliography does not include the myriad reprintings of his magazine and newspaper pieces in other sources--a virtually impossible task considering that, as John Wesley Fuller first pointed out in his unpublished dissertation "Prose Styles in the Essays of E. B. White" (University of Washington, 1959), White has been included in more anthologies, readers, and literature texts than any other American writer; an exception has been made, however, in the case of material that is easier to locate in a reprinted source than in the original place of publication.

The bibliography attempts to cover everything White is known to have published, from a short story in 1914 to his most recent book, Essays of E. B. White, in 1977. Much of what he wrote was not by-lined and hence impossible to track down--as when he served as a reporter for the Cornell Daily Sun, the Seattle Times, and the Post-Intelligencer (he substituted for a reporter who was on vacation during a week in 1923). In his study of E. B. White in the Twayne United States Author Series (1974), Edward C. Sampson mentions that White "remembers publishing something--a poem, he thinks--around 1910 in 'The Ladies' Home Journal.'" A page by page search through that magazine for a five year period (1908 to 1912) failed to turn up anything; the bulk of the magazine's unsolicited contributions were unsigned. Indeed, a great deal of White's material was unsigned--the "Notes and Comment" columns and the "Talk of the Town" pieces, for instance--or appeared under a variety of pseudonyms. All unsigned or pseudonymously written material that can be definitely attributed to White has been included; the pseudonyms are given at the end of the entries.

The bibliography is divided into two parts: the first part consists of a listing of White's writings; the second, a listing of material of critical and biographical interest about White and reviews of his books. The entries are arranged chronologically by year, month, day. When more than one item appears in a periodical on the same date, the items are listed by page sequence. Monthly magazines are treated as if they appeared on the first day of the month. Books and pamphlets are listed at the end of the year. When an asterisk appears at the end of an entry, it means that the piece appeared in the Out-of-Town edition of *The New Yorker*; from October 5, 1929 to April 2, 1960, the magazine published both a New York edition and an Out-of-Town edition, and the page numbering was not always the same. I have seen every item listed in part one and all but a half dozen reviews in part two. So-called reviews which turned out to be nothing but brief annotations have not been included.

I wish to acknowledge a substantial debt to many people who helped me. To E. B. White and the late Katharine S. White for generously answering my questions and giving me several valuable leads; to Mrs. Harriet Walden and Mrs. Helen L. Stark of *The New Yorker* for granting me access to *The New Yorker's* library and furnishing me with needed information; to Mr. Jack Howell for his expert advice and wise counsel; to Ms. Tamara Chernow and Ms. Paula Ebbitt for their excellent assistance with part two; to Ms. Scharline F. Howell for her gracious help with the index; to Dr. Juan R. Freudenthal of the Simmons College School of Library Science for his cooperation; to Mr. Boyd Edmonston of the Simmons College Library for his kind help in securing material; to the Emily Hollowell Research Fund; and, finally, to my wife, Victoria, without whom nothing would be possible, for patiently typing the manuscript and helping me at every stage in its preparation.

A. J. Anderson,
School of Library Science,
Simmons College,
Boston, Massachusetts

Part I

Writings by E. B. White

BOOKS AND PAMPHLETS

Is Sex Necessary? or, Why You Feel the Way You Do. New York: Harper & Brothers, 1929. With James Thurber. E. B. White wrote the "Foreword," Chapters 2, 4, 6, 8, and "Answers to Hard Questions."

________. New York: Harper, 1950. With a new introduction by E. B. White.

The Lady Is Cold. New York: Harper & Brothers, 1929.

Ho Hum; Newsbreaks from "The New Yorker." Illustrations by O. Soglow. New York: Farrar & Rinehart, 1931. White selected the "newsbreaks," wrote the tags, or headlines, and provided a Foreword.

Another Ho Hum; More Newsbreaks from "The New Yorker." Illustrations by O. Soglow. New York: Farrar & Rinehart, 1932. White again selected the breaks, wrote the tags or headlines, and provided a Foreword.

Alice Through the Cellophane. New York: John Day Company, 1933. (John Day Pamphlets, No. 26.)

Everyday Is Saturday. New York: Harper & Brothers, 1934.

Farewell to Model T. New York: G. P. Putnam's Sons, 1936.

The Fox of Peapack, and Other Poems. New York: Harper & Brothers, 1938.

Quo Vadimus? or, The Case for the Bicycle. New York: Harper & Brothers, 1939.

A Subtreasury of American Humor. Edited by E. B. White and Katharine S. White. "Introduction" by E. B. White. New York: Coward-MacCann, 1941.

One Man's Meat. New York: Harper & Brothers, 1942.

________. New York: Harper & Brothers, 1944. A new and enlarged edition.

________. New York: Harper, 1950. With an "Introduction" by Morris Bishop. (Harper's Modern Classics.)

Stuart Little. New York: Harper & Brothers, 1945. Pictures by Garth Williams.

World Government and Peace: Selected Notes and Comment, 1943-1945. New York: F. R. Publishing Corp., 1945. (Reprinted from The New Yorker.)

The Wild Flag: Editorials from the New Yorker on Federal World Government and Other Matters. Boston: Houghton Mifflin, 1946.

Here Is New York. New York: Harper & Brothers, 1949.

Charlotte's Web. New York: Harper, 1952. Pictures by Garth Williams.

The Second Tree from the Corner. New York: Harper, 1954.

________. New York: Harper, 1962. With Critical and Biographical Material by William W. Watt. (Harper's Modern Classics.)

The Elements of Style by William Strunk, Jr. With Revisions, an Introduction, and a New Chapter on Writing by E. B. White. New York: Macmillan, 1959.

________. New York: Macmillan, 1972. Contains a slightly different introduction.

The Points of My Compass: Letters from the East, the West, the North, the South. New York: Harper & Row, 1962.

An E. B. White Reader. New York: Harper & Row, 1966. Edited with Commentary and Questions by William W. Watt and Robert W. Bradford.

The Trumpet of the Swan. New York: Harper & Row, 1970. Pictures by Edward Frascino.

Letters of E. B. White. New York: Harper & Row, 1976. Edited by Dorothy Lobrano Guth.

Essays of E. B. White. New York: Harper & Row, 1977. Selected by E. B. White.

VERSE

1916

"How to Study Effectively," High School Oracle (Mount Vernon, N.Y.), XVI (December, 1916), 15.

1917

"A Modern Hiawatha," High School Oracle (Mount Vernon, N.Y.), XVII (April, 1917), 4-6.

1921

"The Bowling Green: To My Dog, Leaving Me," New York Evening Post, June 9, 1921, p. 8.

"The Bowling Green: Press Service," New York Evening Post, October 15, 1921, p. 10.

"The Bowling Green: To the Woolworth Building," New York Evening Post, November 30, 1921, p. 8.

1922

"The Bowling Green: Child's," New York Evening Post, January 21, 1922, p. 8.

"The Bowling Green: In a Deceased Doughnut Factory," New York Evening Post, March 4, 1922, p. 8.

"To Morvich, Winner," The Louisville Herald, May 14, 1922, p. 1.

"The Bowling Green: To Hotspur, Departed," New York Evening Post, October 25, 1922, p. 6.

1923

"The Bowling Green: Bantam and I," New York Evening Post, November 17, 1923, p. 10.

1924

"The Conning Tower: Bok Ballot Ballad," The New York World, January 10, 1924, p. 15.

"The Conning Tower: Tuning in Through Georgia," The New York World, February 11, 1924, p. 9.

"The Conning Tower: The Hotel Anthology," The New York World, February 14, 1924, p. 13.

"The Conning Tower: Paradise Lost: Book IV," The New York World, March 25, 1924, p. 11.

"The Conning Tower: Where Welcome Waits," The New York World, April 4, 1924, p. 11.

"The Conning Tower: In Re Gladness," The New York World, July 7, 1924, p. 11.

"The Conning Tower: In a Garden," The New York World, August 30, 1924, p. 9.

"The Conning Tower: A Young Advertising Man, After a Hard Day at the Office, Writes to the Girl He Loves," The New York World, September 5, 1924, p. 11.

1925

"The Conning Tower: Jury Duty," The New York World, January 19, 1925, p. 13.

"The Conning Tower: To F. P. A., Who Finds Kansas Scenery Dull," The New York World, March 11, 1925, p. 13.

"The Conning Tower: Amor Soporus," The New York World, March 12, 1925, p. 9.

"The Conning Tower: Directions for Burying Me," The New York World, April 24, 1925, p. 13.

"The Conning Tower: New York Child's Garden of Voices," The New York World, October 1, 1925, p. 17.

"The Conning Tower: Returning," The New York World, October 2, 1925, p. 13.

"Definitions: Critic," The New Yorker, I (October 17, 1925), 8.

"Definitions: Commuter," The New Yorker, I (October 24, 1925), 33.

"Definitions: Corset," The New Yorker, I (November 7, 1925), 12.

"Definitions: Prude," The New Yorker, I (November 14, 1925), 27.

"Our Captious Readers," The New Yorker, I (November 14, 1925), 31.

"Subway People," The New Yorker, I (December 5, 1925), 30.

1926

"The Conning Tower: Ritual for a Restaurant," The New York World, January 8, 1926, p. 13.

"The Conning Tower: Coldly, to the Bronze Bust of Holly in Washington Square," The New York World, March 12, 1926, p. 13.

"Crocus," The New Yorker, II (March 20, 1926), 36. (Unsigned)

"The Conning Tower: The Circus," The New York World, April 22, 1926, p. 15.

"The Conning Tower: Shenandoah Road," The New York World, May 31, 1926, p. 13.

"Journeys," The New Yorker, II (June 5, 1926), 22.

"Hot, Carnivorous Retort to Health Food Menu," The New Yorker, II (June 19, 1926), 52.

"The Conning Tower: For Things That Are a Part of Me," The New York World, July 13, 1926, p. 15.

"There's a Tower in the Sky...," The New Yorker, II (July 31, 1926), 17.

"Ruins," The New Yorker, II (August 28, 1926), 18.

"Lawn Dance," The New Yorker, II (September 4, 1926), 18.

"The Conning Tower: September Rain," The New York World, September 9, 1926, p. 13.

"Portrait of a Poet at the Dome," The New Yorker, II (September 11, 1926), 64.

"Eastern Standard," The New Yorker, II (September 25, 1926), 26.

"The Conning Tower: Augury," The New York World, November 16, 1926, p. 13.

"From an Office," The New Yorker, II (November 20, 1926), 29.

"The Conning Tower: Alternatives," The New York World, December 21, 1926, p. 13.

1927

"A Library Lion Speaks," The New Yorker, II (January 8, 1927), 27.

"Marble-Top," The New Yorker, II (January 15, 1927), 21.

"Real Estate," The New Yorker, II (January 22, 1927), 26.

"Tubes," The New Yorker, II (February 5, 1927), 81.

"The Doctor," The New Yorker, II (February 5, 1927), 83.

"Clinic Joust," The New Yorker, III (March 5, 1927), 30.

"The Conning Tower: Expectancy," The New York World, March 18, 1927, p. 13.

"Words," The New Yorker, III (March 19, 1927), 23.

"The Gag Man Has a Horrid Dream," The New Yorker, III (April 2, 1927), 105.

"Five o'Clock," The New Yorker, III (April 16, 1927), 24.

"Lunch Hour," The New Yorker, III (May 21, 1927), 95.

"Love in a Garden," The New Yorker, III (July 2, 1927), 24.

"City Evening," The New Yorker, III (August 6, 1927), 15.

"Soprano," The New Yorker, III (August 6, 1927), 57. (Unsigned)

"The Conning Tower: Program," The New York World, August 26, 1927, p. 11.

"Lullaby for a City Baby," The New Yorker, III (November 19, 1927), 35.

"The Conning Tower: Discovery," The New York World, November 25, 1927, p. 9.

"The Conning Tower: To the Memory of Hotspur, a Model 'T'," The New York World, December 1, 1927, p. 13.

"The Conning Tower: Algernon Charles Swinburne, Slightly Cock-Eyed, Sees the Old Year Out," The New York World, December 29, 1927, p. 13.

1928

"Belated Christmas Card," The New Yorker, III (January 7, 1928), 24.

"Notes from a Desk Calendar," The New Yorker, III (January 14, 1928), 23. (Signed "Beppo.")

"The Conning Tower: Nugatory," The New York World, February 8, 1928, p. 11.

"Intimations at Fifty-Eighth Street," The New Yorker, III (February 11, 1928), 23.

"To a Hot Water Bottle Named Jonathan," The New Yorker, III (February 18, 1928), 28.

"Gramercy Park," The New Yorker, IV (March 3, 1928), 27.

"The Conning Tower: The Spirit of St. Christopher," The New York World, March 8, 1928, p. 13.

"Sunday," The New Yorker, IV (March 10, 1928), 31.

"Cows Wit Wings," The New Yorker, IV (March 17, 1928), 29.

"The Conning Tower: Affidavit in Platitudes," The New York World, April 12, 1928, p. 13.

"Ballad of Little Faith," The New Yorker, IV (April 28, 1928), 24.

"Song for Before Breakfast," The New Yorker, IV (May 5, 1928), 32.

"The Conning Tower: The Plan," The New York World, May 11, 1928, p. 11.

"Natura in Urbe," The New Yorker, IV (May 26, 1928), 26.

"Song to Be Disregarded," The New Yorker, IV (June 2, 1928), 31.

"The Conning Tower: Ol' Man North River," The New York World, June 5, 1928, p. 13.

"Sitting Song," The New Yorker, IV (June 9, 1928), 24.

"Navigation," The New Yorker, IV (July 14, 1928), 21.

"The Conning Tower: Intimations--Not of Immortality," The New York World, August 9, 1928, p. 11.

"The Conning Tower: Soliloquy at Times Square," The New York World, August 20, 1928, p. 11.

"The Conning Tower: To a Lady Across the Way," The New York World, August 24, 1928, p. 11.

"Imperial Airways," The New Yorker, IV (August 25, 1928), 25.

"The Conning Tower: Ontario," The New York World, September 26, 1928, p. 13.

"The Conning Tower: Road by a River," The New York World, October 5, 1928, p. 13.

"To a Lady Who Was Once a Freshman," The New Yorker, IV (October 13, 1928), 25.

"The Conning Tower: Of Things That Are," The New York World, November 7, 1928, p. 11.

"The Conning Tower: This Is a Prayer Before I Sleep," The New York World, December 4, 1928, p. 15.

1929

"The Conning Tower: Rhyme for a Reasonable Lady," The New York World, January 4, 1929, p. 15.

"Sonnet," The New Yorker, IV (February 2, 1929), 19.

"The Courageous One," The New Yorker, V (March 23, 1929), 22.

"Poet, or, The Growth of a Literary Figure," The New Yorker, V (April 6, 1929), 26.

"I Want to Be Insured by Calvin Coolidge," The New Yorker, V (April 20, 1929), 36.

"The Conning Tower: Hail Britannia Our Eye," The New York World, May 31, 1929, p. 15.

"Essences," The New Yorker, V (July 6, 1929), 18.

"The Conning Tower: Variant," The New York World, October 7, 1929, p. 15.

"The Conning Tower: The Twentieth Century Gets Through," The New York World, December 4, 1929, p. 13.

"The Fox of Peapack," The New Yorker, V (December 7, 1929), 29.

1930

"The Conning Tower: Trees of Winter," The New York World, January 9, 1930, p. 15.

"Lines for an Amaryllis Keeper," The New Yorker, V (January 11, 1930), 26.

"For Serena, Who Owns a Pair of Snowshoes," The New Yorker, V (February 1, 1930), 20.

"The Driving of the Rivet," The New Yorker, V (February 15, 1930), 21.

"The Conning Tower: For Serena, Keeper of the Draw-Curtains," The New York World, February 18, 1930, p. 13.

"Translations from the Calvinese," The New Yorker, VI (April 19, 1930), 22.

"The Conning Tower: Traveler's Song," The New York World, June 10, 1930, p. 11.

"The Conning Tower: To Serena on a September Day," The New York World, September 18, 1930, p. 13.

"They Have Never Kept a Secret from Us Yet," The New Yorker, VI (October 4, 1930), 24.

"To a Perhaps Unavoidably Late Rose," The New Yorker, VI (October 11, 1930), 28.

"A Man I Saw," The New Yorker, VI (October 18, 1930), 24.

"Book Review," The New Yorker, VI (October 25, 1930), 26.

"Dog Around the Block," The New Yorker, VI (December 6, 1930), 27.

"Book Review," The New Yorker, VI (December 13, 1930), 26.

1931

"The Conning Tower: And If One Had a Kennel One Might

Call It a Dog Den So That It Might Remind One of Ogden," The New York World, February 6, 1931, p. 15.

"The Conning Tower: Apostrophe in a Pram Rider," The New York World, February 11, 1931, p. 13.

"The Timid Nautilus," The New Yorker, VII (March 28, 1931), 24.

"Psalm of David Smith," The New Yorker, VII (April 11, 1931), 28.

"Book Review," The New Yorker, VII (May 23, 1931), 14.*

"A Father Does His Best," The New Yorker, VII (June 20, 1931), 18.*

"Colonel Woodcock's Caller," The New Yorker, VII (September 19, 1931), 27.

"The Conning Tower: Before Breakfast," The New York Herald Tribune, October 14, 1931, p. 21.

"Harvest of Half-Truths," The New Yorker, VII (November 28, 1931), 20.

1932

"The Conning Tower: Meridian Seven," The New York Herald Tribune, January 20, 1932, p. 15.

"Song for the Delegates," The New Yorker, VII (January 23, 1932), 18.

"Love," The New Yorker, VII (February 13, 1932), 58.

"To a Perfumed Lady at the Concert," The New Yorker, VIII (March 19, 1932), 23.*

"The Conning Tower: The Shaw-Terry Letters," The New York Herald Tribune, April 14, 1932, p. 15.

"The Conning Tower: Complicated Thoughts about a Small Son," The New York Herald Tribune, May 12, 1932, p. 17.

"The Conning Tower: Money in the Bank Helps Not The [sic]," The New York Herald Tribune, May 27, 1932, p. 19.

"Song from an X-Ray Table," The New Yorker, VIII (August 13, 1932), 13.

"Memo for an Unclaimed Pad," The New Yorker, VIII (August 27, 1932), 23.

"The Conning Tower: Last Day," The New York Herald Tribune, November 2, 1932, p. 17.

"Harper to Mifflin to Chance," The New Yorker, VIII (December 10, 1932), 21.

1933

"The Conning Tower: Notes for a New Whirl Symphony," The New York Herald Tribune, January 11, 1933, p. 17.

"Memorandum for an Infant Boy," The New Yorker, VIII (January 14, 1933), 18.

"First Night," The New Yorker, VIII (February 4, 1933), 23.

"Simples for Cabinet Members," The New Yorker, IX (March 4, 1933), 19.

"The Conning Tower: Origins," The New York Herald Tribune, March 7, 1933, p. 11.

"Ballade of Meaty Inversions," The New Yorker, IX (March 11, 1933), 18.

"The Conning Tower: Street Corner on a Lesser Doomsday," The New York Herald Tribune, April 25, 1933, p. 11.

"So I Ups to Morgan," The New Yorker, IX (April 29, 1933), 25.

"I Paint What I See," The New Yorker, IX (May 20, 1933), 25.

"Question, More or Less Direct," The New Yorker, IX (July 22, 1933), 14.

"Come, Sweet Culture, Prithee Come!" The New Yorker, IX (September 30, 1933), 24.

"The Conning Tower: Verse Sweetens Toil," The New York Herald Tribune, October 3, 1933, p. 19.

"A Connecticut Lad," The New Yorker, IX (October 14, 1933), 29.

"Jungle Flower," The New Yorker, IX (November 18, 1933), 24.

"Book Review," The New Yorker, IX (December 16, 1933), 27.

1934

"The Mall," The New Yorker, IX (January 13, 1934), [xx] (Unsigned)

"The Conning Tower: Statement of the Foreign Policy of One Citizen of the United States," The New York Herald Tribune, January 29, 1934, p. 9.

"Lines Long after Santayana," The New Yorker, IX (February 3, 1934), 21.

"The Iron Man," The New Yorker, X (March 10, 1934), 20.

"The Conning Tower: Dinner in Virginia," The New York Herald Tribune, April 13, 1934, p. 15.

"The Law of the Jungle," The New Yorker, X (April 14, 1934), 31.

"Down with Cake," The New Yorker, X (May 12, 1934), 22.

"The Silence of the Gears," The New Yorker, X (May 19, 1934), 23.

"Holidays Are Sad Days for People Who Don't Have Holidays," The New Yorker, X (May 26, 1934), 20.

"Underground Resistances," The New Yorker, X (June 9, 1934), 25.

"A General Survey of Early Summer in Town and Country," The New Yorker, X (June 23, 1934), 17.

"Apostrophic Notes from the New-World Physics," The New Yorker, X (October 6, 1934), 24.

"The Conning Tower: Thankless Guest Exposes Lyric Host," The New York Herald Tribune, October 8, 1934, p. 11.

"The Conning Tower: The Life of Spice," The New York Herald Tribune, October 12, 1934, p. 27.

"Is a Train," The New Yorker, X (October 27, 1934), 26.

"Ballad of Lost Standing," The New Yorker, X (November 17, 1934), 21.*

"Observation," The New Yorker, X (December 29, 1934), 16.*

1935

"Sequoia, How Oya?" The New Yorker, XI (March 9, 1935), 17.*

"The Conning Tower: To an Outstanding Woman," The New York Herald Tribune, March 12, 1935, p. 15.

"Thoughts on Where to Live," The New Yorker, XI (May 4, 1935), 25.*

"Spain in Fifty-Ninth Street," The New Yorker, XI (June 15, 1935), 14.*

"Hail to Franklin D. Roosevelt," The New Yorker, XI (October 19, 1935), 30.*

"The Conning Tower: A Contrib, to His Sweet Master," The New York Herald Tribune, November 7, 1935, p. 21.

"Chemistry," The New Yorker, XI (November 9, 1935), 21.*

"Hymn to the Dark," The New Yorker, XI (November 23, 1935), 23.*

"Carrousel," The New Yorker, XI (December 21, 1935), 25.*

1936

"The Conning Tower: Clarence Day," The New York Herald Tribune, January 4, 1936, p. 13.

"That Goes for You, Siegfried," The New Yorker, XI (January 25, 1936), 25.*

"It's Spring, Spring in Pittsfield, Mass.," The New Yorker, XII (March 28, 1936), 30.*

"The Conning Tower: World Girdling," The New York Herald Tribune, October 19, 1936, p. 15.

"Hawthorn Hill," The New Yorker, XII (November 28, 1936), 22.*

"The Conning Tower: The King and His Ladye," The New York Herald Tribune, December 7, 1936, p. 15.

"Fashions in Dogs," The New Yorker, XII (December 19, 1936), 27.*

1937

"Pigeon, Sing Cuccu!" The New Yorker, XIII (April 10, 1937), 27.*

"I Say to You, Cheerio," The New Yorker, XIII (May 22, 1937), 18.*

"Flying Over Ethiopian Mountain Ranges," The New Yorker, XIII (December 11, 1937), 26.*

1938

"The Passionate Passenger to His Love," The New Yorker, XIII (February 12, 1938), 24.*

"A Despot's Got to Think of Everything," The New Yorker, XIII (February 12, 1938), 44.*

"In Gallipolis the Bells are Tolling," The New Yorker, XIV (March 5, 1938), 27.*

"An Earthbound Boy," The New Yorker, XIV (May 21, 1938), 29.*

"Card of Greeting," The New Yorker, XIV (December 24, 1938), 20.*

1939

"Peskiness and Peace," The New Yorker, XV (August 26, 1939), 17.*

1940

"The Snood and Its Relation to Me," The New Yorker, XVI (April 13, 1940), 16.*

1941

"Orange Juice," The New Yorker, XVII (February 22, 1941), 24.*

"The Well-Shod Boy," The New Yorker, XVII (October 4, 1941), 27.*

"Inner-Spring Mattresses," The New Yorker, XVII (October 18, 1941), 28.*

1942

"Song of the Middle Years," The New Yorker, XVIII (December 19, 1942), 28.

1943

"Bellum in Medium Bellum," The New Yorker, XIX (July 17, 1943), 56.

1944

"The Sinking of the Scharnhorst," The New Yorker, XIX (January 8, 1944), 23.

"Home Song," The New Yorker, XIX (February 5, 1944), 30.

"A Classic Waits for Me," The New Yorker, XX (February 19, 1944), 25.

"The Shoppers," The New Yorker, XX (April 22, 1944), 29.

"Husbands and Wives," The New Yorker, XX (June 3, 1944), 26.

"Vermin," The New Yorker, XX (October 7, 1944), 22.

"Village Revisited," The New Yorker, XX (December 9, 1944), 30.

1945

"Bells into Box," The New Yorker, XX (January 6, 1945), 22.

"Pearl Harbor Investigation," The New Yorker, XXI (December 8, 1945), 34.*

"Song of the Queen Bee," The New Yorker, XXI (December 15, 1945), 37.*

1946

"Window Ledge in the Atom Age," The New Yorker, XXII (February 23, 1946), 36.

"The Red Cow Is Dead," The New Yorker, XXII (June 1, 1946), 30.

"The Muse and the Mug," The New Yorker, XXII (November 2, 1946), 38.

"Under a Steamer Rug," The New Yorker, XXII (November 30, 1946), 38.

1947

"Love Among the Foreign Offices," The New Yorker, XXII (February 1, 1947), 24.

"To the Princess on Her Birthday," The New Yorker, XXIII (May 3, 1947), 38.

"Abercrombie's Deep-Tangled Wildwood," The New Yorker, XXIII (June 14, 1947), 28.

"No Matter What the Skirt Length Is, Every Prospect Pleases Me, Because I Am Vile," The New Yorker, XXIII (November 1, 1947), 31.

1948

"Conch," The New Yorker, XXIV (April 24, 1948), 33.

"Books: Malabar Farm by Louis Bromfield," The New Yorker, XXIV (May 8, 1948), 104.

"A Forward Glance O'er the Obituary Page," The New Yorker, XXIV (August 28, 1948), 20.

"Card of Thanks," The New Yorker, XXIV (November 13, 1948), 29.

"I Spy," The New Yorker, XXIV (December 18, 1948), 30.

1949

"The Amiable Nonentity," The New Yorker, XXV (March 26, 1949), 92.

"Pasture Management," The New Yorker, XXV (July 30, 1949), 32.

"Boston Is Like No Other Place in the World Only More So," The New Yorker, XXV (October 1, 1949), 32.

1950

"Stand Down, Ye Pusillanimous Rascals!" The New Yorker, XXVI (April 29, 1950), 32.

"Sinkside Reverie," The New Yorker, XXVI (May 27, 1950), 28.

"Thoughts While Sowing Five Pounds of Domestic Rye Grass Seed at 40 Cents the Pound," The New Yorker, XXVI (September 23, 1950), 38.

1951

"Message: To Be Dropped Inside Russia from a Gas Balloon," The New Yorker, XXVII (June 2, 1951), 34.

1952

"I Am Dying to Know What You Are Saying, Egypt," The New Yorker, XXVII (January 19, 1952), 26.

"Springtime Crossroad Episode in Four-Time," The New Yorker, XXVIII (April 5, 1952), 40.

"The Answer Is 'No'," The New Yorker, XXVIII (December 20, 1952), 38.

1953

"The ABC of Security," The New Yorker, XXIX (May 9, 1953), 36.

1955

"Palace Thoughts," The New Yorker, XXXI (March 12, 1955), 102.

"Ever Popular Am I, Mammoth, Wilt Resistant," The New Yorker, XXXI (March 26, 1955), 36.

"The Passing of Alpheus W. Halliday," The New Yorker, XXXI (December 24, 1955), 19.*

1956

"The Feet of the Mayor of Clay," The New Yorker, XXXIII (September 29, 1956), 32.

"The Tennis," The New Yorker, XXXII (October 6, 1956), 46.

1957

"A Table for One," The New Yorker, XXXIII (February 23, 1957), 38.

"Lines," The New Yorker, XXXIII (August 31, 1957), 32.

1958

"The Misstep," The New Yorker, XXXIV (July 12, 1958), 28.

1959

"A Listener's Guide to the Birds," The New Yorker, XXXV (July 4, 1959), 28-29.

1961

"The Unwinding," The New Yorker, XXXVII (June 24, 1961), 24.

1963

"Burdens of High Office," The New Yorker, XXXIX (October 12, 1963), 56.

1966

"The Deserted Nation," The New Yorker, XLII (October 8, 1966), 53.

1967

"Survival Through Adaptation," The New Yorker, XLIII (April 15, 1967), 50.

1969

"Chairs in Snow," The New Yorker, XLV (April 12, 1969), 44.

ARTICLES, SHORT STORIES, AND OTHER PROSE PIECES

1914

"A True Dog Story," St. Nicholas, XLI (September, 1914), 1045.

1916

"Pink Hats," High School Oracle (Mount Vernon, N.Y.), XVI (March, 1916), 3-6.

"All for Xmas," High School Oracle (Mount Vernon, N.Y.), XVI (December, 1916), 11-14.

1921

"The Manuscript Club," The Cornell Era, LIII (June 11, 1921), 9.

"The Bowling Green: If You Say So," New York Evening Post, December 8, 1921, p. 8.

1925

"A Step Forward," The New Yorker, I (April 18, 1925), 21.

"Defense of the Bronx River," The New Yorker, I (May 9, 1925), 14.

"Why I Like New York," The New Yorker, I (August 22, 1925), 10.

"Why I Like New York," The New Yorker, I (October 10, 1925), 31.

"Definitions: Clergyman," The New Yorker, I (November 14, 1925), 35.

"Child's Play," The New Yorker, I (December 26, 1925), 17.

1926

"Always," The New Yorker, II (May 8, 1926), 31.

"Lower Level," The New Yorker, II (May 22, 1926), 20.

"Poco Agitato," The New Yorker, II (May 29, 1926), 57-58.

"Garter Motif," The New Yorker, II (June 5, 1926), 33.

"The Light That Failed," The New Yorker, II (July 17, 1926), 16.

"Hey Day Labor," The New Yorker, II (August 7, 1926), 21.

"The Swell Steerage," The New Yorker, II (August 14, 1926), 20.

"Getting Through the Day," The New Yorker, II (August 28, 1926), 13-14.

"Petit Dejeuner," The New Yorker, II (September 18, 1926), 26.

"The Receiving Line," The New Yorker, II (September 25, 1926), 21.

"The Talk of the Town: Notes and Comment," The New Yorker, II (October 2, 1926), 17.

"Renting the Leviathan," The New Yorker, II (October 2, 1926), 50-51.

"Life Cycle of a Literary Genius," The New Yorker, II (October 16, 1926), 31.

"A Lady of the Chorus Watches Dorothy Stone," The New Yorker, II (October 30, 1926), 29.

"The Little Man," The New Yorker, II (November 6, 1926), 22-23.

"Construction," The New Yorker, II (November 6, 1926), 48.

"No Hat," The New Yorker, II (November 27, 1926), 28.

"The Talk of the Town: Notes and Comment," The New Yorker, II (December 4, 1926), 23.

"Elevated," The New Yorker, II (December 4, 1926), 107.

"What, Ma, No Jam?" The New Yorker, II (December 11, 1926), 35.

"Open Letter to My Burgler," The New Yorker, II (December 11, 1926), 52-54.

"Exploration," The New Yorker, II (December 11, 1926), 93.

"Lines in Anguish," The New Yorker, II (December 11, 1926), 113.

"The Talk of the Town: Notes and Comment," The New Yorker, II (December 18, 1926), 19.

1927

"The Talk of the Town: Notes and Comment," The New Yorker, II (January 1, 1927), 7.

"The Talk of the Town: Harbinger," The New Yorker, II (January 1, 1927), 8.

"Upside Down," The New Yorker, II (January 1, 1927), 19-20.

"The Talk of the Town: Notes and Comment," The New Yorker, II (January 8, 1927), 13.

"The Talk of the Town: Ringing Steel," The New Yorker, II (January 15, 1927), 9.

"No Reply Yet, Or Undank Ist Der Welt-Lohn," The New Yorker, II (January 15, 1927), 17.

"The Talk of the Town: Notes and Comment," The New Yorker, II (January 22, 1927), 9.

"Before Baby Came," The New Yorker, II (January 22, 1927), 15.

"Lopsided," The New Yorker, II (January 22, 1927), 23.

"The Talk of the Town: Notes and Comment," The New Yorker, II (January 29, 1927), 17.

"The Talk of the Town: Notes and Comment," The New Yorker, II (February 5, 1927), 17.

"The Talk of the Town: One Year Old," The New Yorker, II (February 5, 1927), 19.

"M'Baby Loves Me," The New Yorker, II (February 5, 1927), 30.

"The Talk of the Town: Notes and Comment," The New Yorker, II (February 12, 1927), 17.

"The Talk of the Town: Royal," The New Yorker, II (February 12, 1927), 19.

"The Talk of the Town: Notes and Comment," The New Yorker, III (February 19, 1927), 17-18.

"The Talk of the Town: Hammer," The New Yorker, III (February 19, 1927), 19.

"Why Albert Ferncroft Is a Bitter Man," The New Yorker, III (February 19, 1927), 28.

"The Talk of the Town: Notes and Comment," The New Yorker, III (February 26, 1927), 17.

"The Talk of the Town: Notes and Comment," The New Yorker, III (March 5, 1927), 17.

"The Talk of the Town: Notes and Comment," The New Yorker, III (March 12, 1927), 17.

"The Talk of the Town: Notes and Comment," The New Yorker, III (March 19, 1927), 17.

"The Talk of the Town: Predatory," The New Yorker, III (March 19, 1927), 21.

"An Evening on Ice," The New Yorker, III (March 19, 1927), 30.

"The Talk of the Town: Notes and Comment," The New Yorker, III (March 26, 1927), 17.

"The Mexican Suit," The New Yorker, III (March 26, 1927), 40-44.

"The Talk of the Town: Notes and Comment," The New Yorker, III (April 2, 1927), 17.

"Mate-of-the-Month Club," The New Yorker, III (April 2, 1927), 30.

"The Talk of the Town: Notes and Comment," The New Yorker, III (April 9, 1927), 17.

"Interview with a Sparrow," The New Yorker, III (April 9, 1927), 31.

"The Talk of the Town: Notes and Comment," The New Yorker, III (April 16, 1927), 17.

"The Talk of the Town: Winter into Spring," The New Yorker, III (April 16, 1927), 20.

"The Talk of the Town: Notes and Comment," The New Yorker, III (April 23, 1927), 17.

"America," The New Yorker, III (April 23, 1927), 23-24.

"The Talk of the Town: Notes and Comment," The New Yorker, III (April 30, 1927), 17.

"The Talk of the Town: Notes and Comment," The New Yorker, III (May 7, 1927), 13.

"The Talk of the Town: Notes and Comment," The New Yorker, III (May 14, 1927), 13.

"Couple," The New Yorker, III (May 14, 1927), 94-95.

"The Talk of the Town: Notes and Comment," The New Yorker, III (May 21, 1927), 13.

"The Talk of the Town: Yachts," The New Yorker, III (May 21, 1927), 17.

"Things That Bother Me," The New Yorker, III (May 21, 1927), 19.

"The Talk of the Town: Notes and Comment," The New Yorker, III (May 28, 1927), 11.

"The Talk of the Town: Eviction," The New Yorker, III (May 28, 1927), 14.

"The Talk of the Town: Tifft." The New Yorker, III (May 28, 1927), 15.

"The Talk of the Town: Notes and Comment," The New Yorker, III (June 4, 1927), 11.

"The Talk of the Town: Friendly," The New Yorker, III (June 4, 1927), 12.

"Howdy, King; Howdy, Queen," The New Yorker, III (June 4, 1927), 28.

"The Talk of the Town: Notes and Comment," The New Yorker, III (June 11, 1927), 9.

"Rubbing Elbows," The New Yorker, III (June 11, 1927), 23-24.

"The Talk of the Town: Notes and Comment," The New Yorker, III (June 18, 1927), 9-10.

"The Talk of the Town: Horse Mart," The New Yorker, III (June 18, 1927), 10.

"Thoughts--While Minding a Sleeping Infant Belonging to Someone Else," The New Yorker, III (June 18, 1927), 16.

"Suggested Telegrams," The New Yorker, III (June 18, 1927), 26.

"The Talk of the Town: Notes and Comment," The New Yorker, III (June 25, 1927), 9.

"The Talk of the Town: Notes and Comment," The New Yorker, III (July 2, 1927), 9.

"The Talk of the Town: 'We'," The New Yorker, III (July 2, 1927), 12.

"The Talk of the Town: Cold Feet," The New Yorker, III (July 2, 1927), 13.

"The Talk of the Town: Snakes," The New Yorker, III (July 2, 1927), 19.

"The Talk of the Town: Notes and Comment," The New Yorker, III (July 9, 1927), 9.

"The Talk of the Town: Notes and Comment," The New Yorker, III (July 16, 1927), 9.

"The Talk of the Town: Notes and Comment," The New Yorker, III (July 23, 1927), 9.

"The Talk of the Town: Clock Store," The New Yorker, III (July 23, 1927), 10.

"The Talk of the Town: Notes and Comment," The New Yorker, III (July 30, 1927), 7.

"The Talk of the Town: Historic," The New Yorker, III (July 30, 1927), 8.

"The Talk of the Town: Notes and Comment," The New Yorker, III (August 6, 1927), 9-10.

"The Talk of the Town: Celebrities," The New Yorker, III (August 6, 1927), 10.

"Shrine," The New Yorker, III (August 6, 1927), 31.

"The Talk of the Town: Notes and Comment," The New Yorker, III (August 13, 1927), 9.

"Tombs Are Best," The New Yorker, III (August 13, 1927), 14-15.

"The Talk of the Town: Notes and Comment," The New Yorker, III (August 20, 1927), 9.

"How to Be Elegant," The New Yorker, III (August 20, 1927), 25.

"The Talk of the Town: Notes and Comment," The New Yorker, III (August 27, 1927), 9.

"Our Own Controversy," The New Yorker, III (August 27, 1927), 19-20. (Signed "Editors of the New Yorker.")

"The Talk of the Town: Elegant Slums," The New Yorker, III (August 30, 1927), 10.

"The Talk of the Town: Notes and Comment," The New Yorker, III (September 3, 1927), 9.

"The Talk of the Town: Snappy," The New Yorker, III (September 3, 1927), 10.

"Get Rid of New Jersey," The New Yorker, III (September 3, 1927), 15-16.

"The Talk of the Town: Notes and Comment," The New Yorker, III (September 10, 1927), 11.

"The Talk of the Town: Notes and Comment," The New Yorker, III (September 17, 1927), 17.

"The Talk of the Town: Notes and Comment," The New Yorker, III (September 24, 1927), 15.

"Listen, Baby," The New Yorker, III (September 24, 1927), 20.

"The Talk of the Town: Notes and Comment," The New Yorker, III (October 1, 1927), 9.

"Worm Turning," The New Yorker, III (October 1, 1927), 16.

"The Talk of the Town: Notes and Comment," The New Yorker, III (October 8, 1927), 17.

"The Talk of the Town: Professor," The New Yorker, III (October 8, 1927), 19.

"The Talk of the Town: Notes and Comment," The New Yorker, III (October 15, 1927), 17-18.

"Interesting Discovery," The New Yorker, III (October 15, 1927), 34.

"The Talk of the Town: Notes and Comment," The New Yorker, III (October 22, 1927), 13-14.

"Graph Showing Fluctuation in Relations Between France and the United States During Fiscal Good Will Period," The New Yorker, III (October 22, 1927), 19.

"The Talk of the Town: Notes and Comment," The New Yorker, III (October 29, 1927), 13.

"The Talk of the Town: The Boulevard," The New Yorker, III (October 29, 1927), 16.

"The Talk of the Town: Notes and Comment," The New Yorker, III (November 5, 1927), 9.

"Now That I'm Organized," The New Yorker, III (November 5, 1927), 19-20.

"Critique," The New Yorker, III (November 5, 1927), 30.

"The Talk of the Town: Notes and Comment," The New Yorker, III (November 12, 1927), 17-18.

"The Talk of the Town: Way of Living," The New Yorker, III (November 12, 1927), 18.

"There Is No Marion Davies," The New Yorker, III (November 12, 1927), 38.

"The Talk of the Town: Notes and Comment," The New Yorker, III (November 19, 1927), 19.

"The Talk of the Town: Openings," The New Yorker, III (November 19, 1927), 23.

"The Talk of the Town: Notes and Comment," The New Yorker, III (November 25, 1927), 19-20.

"The Talk of the Town: Make-Believe," The New Yorker, III (November 26, 1927), 20.

"The Talk of the Town: Notes and Comment," The New Yorker, III (December 3, 1927), 19-20.

"The Talk of the Town: Free," The New Yorker, III (December 3, 1927), 21.

"The Talk of the Town: Notes and Comment," The New Yorker, III (December 10, 1927), 19.

"The Talk of the Town: Model Oh!," The New Yorker, III (December 10, 1927), 21.

"The Talk of the Town: Notes and Comment," The New Yorker, III (December 17, 1927), 17.

"The Talk of the Town: Notes and Comment," The New Yorker, III (December 24, 1927), 7-8.

"Thoughts While Skating 240 Laps at the Ice Club," The New Yorker, III (December 24, 1927), 15-16.

"The Talk of the Town: Notes and Comment," The New Yorker, III (December 31, 1927), 7.

"The Talk of the Town: What Every Adult Should Know," The New Yorker, III (December 31, 1927), 9.

1928

"The Talk of the Town: Notes and Comment," The New Yorker, III (January 7, 1928), 9-10.

"The Talk of the Town: Notes and Comment," The New Yorker, III (January 14, 1928), 9-10.

"The Talk of the Town: Champs," The New Yorker, III (January 14, 1928), 12.

"The Talk of the Town: Ever Upward," The New Yorker, III (January 21, 1928), 9.

"The Talk of the Town: Notes and Comment," The New Yorker, III (January 21, 1928), 9.

"How to Drive the New Ford," The New Yorker, III (January 21, 1928), 17-18.

"The Talk of the Town: Notes and Comment," The New Yorker, III (January 28, 1928), 9-10.

"The Talk of the Town: With Camera and Cockerel," The New Yorker, III (January 28, 1928), 10.

"The Talk of the Town: Notes and Comment," The New Yorker, III (February 4, 1928), 9-10.

"The Talk of the Town: Rabbi and Judge," The New Yorker, III (February 4, 1928), 10.

"He," The New Yorker, III (February 4, 1928), 19.

"The Talk of the Town: Notes and Comment," The New Yorker, III (February 11, 1928), 9-10.

"The Talk of the Town: Heart Throbs," The New Yorker, III (February 11, 1928), 11.

"The Talk of the Town: Notes and Comment," The New Yorker, III (February 18, 1928), 9.

"The Talk of the Town: Seeing Things," The New Yorker, III (February 18, 1928), 12.

"Pullmanism," The New Yorker, III (February 18, 1928), 24.

"Yours of the Ult., Ours of the Inst.," The New Yorker, III (February 18, 1928), 42-46. (Signed "The Editors.")

"The Talk of the Town: Notes and Comment," The New Yorker, IV (February 25, 1928), 11-12.

"Poets Are Being Watched," The New Yorker, IV (February 25, 1928), 22.

"The Talk of the Town: Notes and Comment," The New Yorker, IV (March 3, 1928), 17-18.

"The Talk of the Town: Mammy India," The New Yorker, IV (March 3, 1928), 19.

"The Talk of the Town: Notes and Comment," The New Yorker, IV (March 10, 1928), 17-18.

"The Talk of the Town: Notes and Comment," The New Yorker, IV (March 17, 1928), 17.

"The Talk of the Town: Ascension," The New Yorker, IV (March 17, 1928), 20.

"Bye Low Baby," The New Yorker, IV (March 17, 1928), 25-26.

"The Talk of the Town: Notes and Comment," The New Yorker, IV (March 24, 1928), 13-14.

"The Talk of the Town: Trader Horn," The New Yorker, IV (March 24, 1928), 14.

"The Talk of the Town: Notes and Comment," The New Yorker, IV (March 31, 1928), 17.

"The Talk of the Town: Air Made Easy," The New Yorker, IV (March 31, 1928), 21.

"The Talk of the Town: Notes and Comment," The New Yorker, IV (April 7, 1928), 17-18.

"The Subway Trouble Explained," The New Yorker, IV (April 7, 1928), 25.

"The Talk of the Town: Notes and Comment," The New Yorker, IV (April 14, 1928), 13-14.

"The Talk of the Town: Notes and Comment," The New Yorker, IV (April 21, 1928), 17.

"The Talk of the Town: Marble from Steel," The New Yorker, IV (April 21, 1928), 19.

"The Talk of the Town: Notes and Comment," The New Yorker, IV (April 28, 1928), 13.

"The Talk of the Town: Notes and Comment," The New Yorker, IV (May 5, 1928), 17.

"The Talk of the Town: Potter's Field," The New Yorker, IV (May 5, 1928), 20.

"The Talk of the Town: Notes and Comment," The New Yorker, IV (May 12, 1928), 15-16.

"Treasures Upon Earth," The New Yorker, IV (May 12, 1928), 22.

"The Talk of the Town: Notes and Comment," The New Yorker, IV (May 19, 1928), 17-18.

"The Talk of the Town: Harriett," The New Yorker, IV (May 19, 1928), 18.

"The Talk of the Town: Notes and Comment," The New Yorker, IV (May 26, 1928), 13.

"The Talk of the Town: Zoo Things," The New Yorker, IV (May 26, 1928), 15.

"The Talk of the Town: Notes and Comment," The New Yorker, IV (June 2, 1928), 17-18.

"The Talk of the Town: Harbor Lady," The New Yorker, IV (June 2, 1928), 19.

"The Talk of the Town: Tea Taster," The New Yorker, IV (June 2, 1928), 21.

"The Talk of the Town: Notes and Comment," The New Yorker, IV (June 9, 1928), 9.

"The Talk of the Town: Notes and Comment," The New Yorker, IV (June 16, 1928), 15.

"The Talk of the Town: 301 Mott," The New Yorker, IV (June 16, 1928), 18.

"The Talk of the Town: Notes and Comment," The New Yorker, IV (June 23, 1928), 7.

"Getting Away," The New Yorker, IV (June 23, 1928), 12.

"The Talk of the Town: Notes and Comment," The New Yorker, IV (June 30, 1928), 9.

"The Talk of the Town: Notes and Comment," The New Yorker, IV (July 7, 1928), 7.

"The Care and Feeding of Begonias, or, The Manly Art," The New Yorker, IV (July 7, 1928), 23.

"The Talk of the Town: Notes and Comment," The New Yorker, IV (July 14, 1928), 13-14.

"The Talk of the Town: Notes and Comment," The New Yorker, IV (July 21, 1928), 9.

"The Talk of the Town: Notes and Comment," The New Yorker, IV (July 28, 1928), 9.

'Montparnasse," The New Yorker, IV (July 28, 1928), 24.

"The Talk of the Town: Notes and Comment," The New Yorker, IV (August 4, 1928), 7.

"Open Letter to the Department of Correction," The New Yorker, IV (August 4, 1928), 21-22.

"The Talk of the Town: Notes and Comment," The New Yorker, IV (August 11, 1928), 11.

"The Talk of the Town: Northern," The New Yorker, IV (August 11, 1928), 12.

"Tunney's Little Man," The New Yorker, IV (August 11, 1928), 20.

"The Talk of the Town: Notes and Comment," The New Yorker, IV (August 18, 1928), 9-10.

"The Talk of the Town: Lonely Hearts," The New Yorker, IV (August 18, 1928), 12.

"The Talk of the Town: A-Fishing Go," The New Yorker, IV (August 18, 1928), 13.

"The Talk of the Town: Notes and Comment," The New Yorker, IV (August 25, 1928), 11.

"The Talk of the Town: Notes and Comment," The New Yorker, IV (September 1, 1928), 9.

"Breakfast with Peers," The New Yorker, IV (September 1, 1928), 18.

"The Talk of the Town: Notes and Comment," The New Yorker, IV (September 8, 1928), 11.

"The Talk of the Town: Notes and Comment," The New Yorker, IV (September 15, 1928), 17.

"The Talk of the Town: Notes and Comment," The New Yorker, IV (September 22, 1928), 13-14.

"The Talk of the Town: Helen," The New Yorker, IV (September 22, 1928), 15.

"The Color of Mice," The New Yorker, IV (September 22, 1928), 19-20.

"The Talk of the Town: Notes and Comment," The New Yorker, IV (September 29, 1928), 15.

"The Talk of the Town: Red Hot Glamour," The New Yorker, IV (September 29, 1928), 17.

"The Talk of the Town: Black Magic," *The New Yorker*, IV (September 29, 1928), 18.

"Memoirs of a Dramatic Critic," *The New Yorker*, IV (September 29, 1928), 23-24.

"The Talk of the Town: Notes and Comment," *The New Yorker*, IV (October 6, 1928), 17.

"The Talk of the Town: Interim," *The New Yorker*, IV (October 6, 1928), 19.

"My Little Cabin Monoplane," *The New Yorker*, IV (October 6, 1928), 36-42.

"The Talk of the Town: Notes and Comment," *The New Yorker*, IV (October 13, 1928), 17.

"The Talk of the Town: Notes and Comment," *The New Yorker*, IV (October 20, 1928), 13-14.

"The Talk of the Town: Suits for Jimmy," *The New Yorker*, IV (October 20, 1928), 14.

"The Talk of the Town: Notes and Comment," *The New Yorker*, IV (October 27, 1928), 17-18.

"The Talk of the Town: Old Clocks," *The New Yorker*, IV (October 27, 1928), 19.

"Where Do the New Eras Go?" *The Magazine of Business*, LIV (November, 1928), 505.

"The Talk of the Town: Notes and Comment," *The New Yorker*, IV (November 3, 1928), 17-18.

"The Talk of the Town: Notes and Comment," *The New Yorker*, IV (November 10, 1928), 17.

"The Talk of the Town: Hoboken Nights," *The New Yorker*, IV (November 10, 1928), 19.

"The Talk of the Town: Notes and Comment," *The New Yorker*, IV (November 17, 1928), 17-18.

"Announcement," *The New Yorker*, IV (November 17, 1928), 23.

"The Talk of the Town: Notes and Comment," The New Yorker, IV (November 24, 1928), 17.

"The Talk of the Town: Flying Over," The New Yorker, IV (November 24, 1928), 20.

"The Talk of the Town: Notes and Comment," The New Yorker, IV (December 1, 1928), 21.

"A Reporter at Large: Sea Beacon," The New Yorker, IV (December 1, 1928), 48-55.

"The Talk of the Town: Notes and Comment," The New Yorker, IV (December 8, 1928), 21-22.

"The Talk of the Town: Sleight of Hand," The New Yorker, IV (December 8, 1928), 22.

"The Talk of the Town: Notes and Comment," The New Yorker, IV (December 15, 1928), 21.

"The Talk of the Town: Fish Wing," The New Yorker, IV (December 15, 1928), 22.

"Rest Room No. 2," The New Yorker, IV (December 15, 1928), 26.

"The Talk of the Town: Notes and Comment," The New Yorker, IV (December 22, 1928), 9-10.

"Open Reply to Mrs. Mendelson," The New Yorker, IV (December 22, 1928), 14.

"The Talk of the Town: Notes and Comment," The New Yorker, IV (December 29, 1928), 9.

"The Talk of the Town: Miniature," The New Yorker, IV (December 29, 1928), 13.

1929

"The Talk of the Town: Notes and Comment," The New Yorker, IV (January 5, 1929), 13.

"The Talk of the Town: Bird Lady," The New Yorker, IV (January 5, 1929), 16.

"It's a 'ome," The New Yorker, IV (January 5, 1929), 18-19. (Signed "Baedeker Jones.")

"The Talk of the Town: Notes and Comment," The New Yorker, IV (January 12, 1929), 9-10.

"The Talk of the Town: Notes for a Ludwig," The New Yorker, IV (January 12, 1929), 13.

"Philip Wedge," The New Yorker, IV (January 12, 1929), 15-16.

"The Talk of the Town: Notes and Comment," The New Yorker, IV (January 19, 1929), 9.

"The Talk of the Town: Civics," The New Yorker, IV (January 19, 1929), 11.

"The Talk of the Town: Notes and Comment," The New Yorker, IV (January 26, 1929), 9-10.

"The Talk of the Town: Notes and Comment," The New Yorker, IV (February 2, 1929), 11-12.

"The Talk of the Town: Notes and Comment," The New Yorker, IV (February 9, 1929), 11.

"O.K. to Go Ahead, or, How Police Horses Are Trained," The New Yorker, IV (February 9, 1929), 18-20. (Signed "Baedeker Jones.")

"The Talk of the Town: Notes and Comment," The New Yorker, IV (February 16, 1929), 11.

"The Talk of the Town: Notes and Comment," The New Yorker, V (February 23, 1929), 11-12.

"The Romance of the Publishing Game," The New Yorker, V (February 23, 1929), 18-19.

"The Talk of the Town: Notes and Comment," The New Yorker, V (March 2, 1929), 13.

"The Talk of the Town: Seeing Shelley Plain," The New Yorker, V (March 2, 1929), 16.

"The Talk of the Town: Notes and Comment," The New Yorker, V (March 9, 1929), 11-12.

"The Talk of the Town: Custom-Cut," The New Yorker, V (March 9, 1929), 12.

"The Talk of the Town: Whee-e!" The New Yorker, V (March 9, 1929), 12.

"The Talk of the Town: Muscles on High," The New Yorker, V (March 9, 1929), 13.

"The Talk of the Town: Notes and Comment," The New Yorker, V (March 16, 1929), 15-16.

"Hotspur the Swift," The New Yorker, V (March 16, 1929), 21.

"The Talk of the Town: Notes and Comment," The New Yorker, V (March 23, 1929), 11-12.

"The Talk of the Town: Destructionist," The New Yorker, V (March 23, 1929), 13.

"The Talk of the Town: Notes and Comment," The New Yorker, V (March 30, 1929), 11.

"West Farm Jottings," The New Yorker, V (March 30, 1929), 74-75. (Signed "Elmer Hostetter.")

"The Talk of the Town: Notes and Comment," The New Yorker, V (April 6, 1929), 17-18.

"The Talk of the Town: Sex Racket," The New Yorker, V (April 6, 1929), 19.

"The Talk of the Town: Span," The New Yorker, V (April 6, 1929), 20.

"Letters We Never Finished Reading: A Selection from the Week's Mail," The New Yorker, V (April 6, 1929), 32.

"The Talk of the Town: Notes and Comment," The New Yorker, V (April 13, 1929), 13.

"The Talk of the Town: Mall," The New Yorker, V (April 13, 1929), 15.

"The Talk of the Town: Round and Round," The New Yorker, V (April 13, 1929), 17.

"Interpretation," The New Yorker, V (April 13, 1929), 27.

"The Talk of the Town: Notes and Comment," The New Yorker, V (April 20, 1929), 13-14.

"The Talk of the Town: War Being Over," The New Yorker, V (April 20, 1929), 16.

"Dream Children: A Reverie," The New Yorker, V (April 20, 1929), 20-21.

"The Talk of the Town: Notes and Comment," The New Yorker, V (April 27, 1929), 13-14.

"The Talk of the Town: Notes and Comment," The New Yorker, V (May 4, 1929), 13-14.

"The Talk of the Town: Birth-Control Hearing," The New Yorker, V (May 4, 1929), 14.

"The Talk of the Town: Rude," The New Yorker, V (May 4, 1929), 17.

"The Talk of the Town: Notes and Comment," The New Yorker, V (May 11, 1929), 11-12.

"The Talk of the Town: Bronx Home News," The New Yorker, V (May 11, 1929), 14.

"The Talk of the Town: Notes and Comment," The New Yorker, V (May 18, 1929), 13.

"The Talk of the Town: Notes and Comment," The New Yorker, V (May 25, 1929), 13-14.

"In Re Life," The Literary Digest, CI (May 25, 1929), 29.

"The Talk of the Town: Notes and Comment," The New Yorker, V (June 1, 1929), 11.

"The Talk of the Town: Notes and Comment," The New Yorker, V (June 8, 1929), 11-12.

"The Talk of the Town: Vestigial Organs," The New Yorker, V (June 8, 1929), 12-14.

"The Talk of the Town: Notes and Comment," The New Yorker, V (June 15, 1929), 11-12.

"The Talk of the Town: Historical," The New Yorker, V (June 15, 1929), 13.

"Casino, I Love You," The New Yorker, V (June 15, 1929), 18-19.

"The Talk of the Town: Notes and Comment," The New Yorker, V (June 22, 1929), 11.

"Baby's First Step," The New Yorker, V (June 22, 1929), 16.

"The Talk of the Town: Notes and Comment," The New Yorker, V (June 29, 1929), 9-10.

"The Talk of the Town: Doormat," The New Yorker, V (June 29, 1929), 11.

"The Talk of the Town: Notes and Comment," The New Yorker, V (July 6, 1929), 9.

"The Wayward Press: Scoops and Denials," The New Yorker, V (July 6, 1929), 26-31. (Signed "S. Finny.")

"The Talk of the Town: Notes and Comment," The New Yorker, V (July 13, 1929), 9-10.

"The Talk of the Town: Notes and Comment," The New Yorker, V (July 20, 1929), 9.

"The Doily Menace," The New Yorker, V (July 20, 1929), 15.

"The Talk of the Town: Cage Delivery," The New Yorker, V (August 3, 1929), 11.

"The Talk of the Town: Notes and Comment," The New Yorker, V (August 10, 1929), 9-10.

"The Talk of the Town: Notes and Comment," The New Yorker, V (August 17, 1929), 9-10.

"The Talk of the Town: Notes and Comment," The New Yorker, V (August 24, 1929), 7.

"The Talk of the Town: Notes and Comment," The New Yorker, V (August 31, 1929), 13.

"The Talk of the Town: Notes and Comment," The New Yorker, V (September 7, 1929), 17-18.

"The Talk of the Town: Notes and Comment," The New Yorker, V (September 14, 1929), 17.

"The Talk of the Town: Notes and Comment," The New Yorker, V (September 21, 1929), 17.

"The Talk of the Town: Runners," The New Yorker, V (September 21, 1929), 21.

"The Talk of the Town: Notes and Comment," The New Yorker, V (September 28, 1929), 17.

"The Talk of the Town: Pastoral," The New Yorker, V (September 28, 1929), 20.

"Frigidity in Men," The New Yorker, V (September 28, 1929), 23-25.

"The Talk of the Town: Notes and Comment," The New Yorker, V (October 5, 1929), 17-18.

"The Talk of the Town: Notes and Comment," The New Yorker, (October 12, 1929), 17-18.

"The Talk of the Town: Notes and Comment," The New Yorker, V (October 19, 1929), 19-20.

"This Is the Girl I'm Going to Marry," The New Yorker, V (October 19, 1929), 28.

"The Talk of the Town: Notes and Comment," The New Yorker, V (October 26, 1929), 21-22.

"The Talk of the Town: Notes and Comment," The New Yorker, V (November 2, 1929), 17.

"The Talk of the Town: Notes and Comment," The New Yorker, V (November 9, 1929), 17-18.

"The Talk of the Town: Notes and Comment," The New Yorker, V (November 16, 1929), 19-20.

"Seeing Gloria Plain," The New Yorker, V (November 16, 1929), 24.

"The Talk of the Town: Notes and Comment," The New Yorker, V (November 23, 1929), 19-20.

"The Talk of the Town: Notes and Comment," The New Yorker, V (November 30, 1929), 17-18.

"What Should Children Tell Parents?" Harper's Magazine, CLX (December, 1929), 120-122.

"The Talk of the Town: Notes and Comment," The New Yorker, V (December 7, 1929), 21-22.

"The Talk of the Town: Isadora's Brother," The New Yorker, V (December 7, 1929), 22.

"The Talk of the Town: Notes and Comment," The New Yorker, V (December 14, 1929), 19-20.

"The Talk of the Town: Notes and Comment," The New Yorker, V (December 21, 1929), 17-18.

"The Talk of the Town: Notes and Comment," The New Yorker, V (December 28, 1929), 9-10.

1930

"Where Are the Diabolos?" The Forum and Century, LXXXIII (January, 1930), 50-52.

"The Talk of the Town: Notes and Comment," The New Yorker, V (January 4, 1930), 11.

"The Talk of the Town: Namesake," The New Yorker, V (January 4, 1930), 13.

"The Talk of the Town: Notes and Comment," The New Yorker, V (January 11, 1930), 11-12.

"Johnson Returns," The New Yorker, V (January 11, 1930), 44-45. (Signed "Fairfax Vinton.")

"The Talk of the Town: Notes and Comment," The New Yorker, V (January 18, 1930), 11-12.

"The Talk of the Town: Notes and Comment," The New Yorker, V (January 25, 1930), 11-12.

"The Talk of the Town: Notes and Comment," The New Yorker, V (February 1, 1930), 9-10.

"The Talk of the Town: Notes and Comment," The New Yorker, V (February 8, 1930), 11.

"The Talk of the Town: Animal Voices," The New Yorker, V (February 8, 1930), 14.

"The Talk of the Town: Ex-Uncle." The New Yorker, V (February 8, 1930), 16. (Signed "Anonymous.")

"The Talk of the Town: Notes and Comment," The New Yorker, V (February 15, 1930), 11.

"The Talk of the Town: Notes and Comment," The New Yorker, VI (February 22, 1930), 17-18.

"The Talk of the Town: Notes and Comment," The New Yorker, VI (March 1, 1930), 11-12.

"The Talk of the Town: Notes and Comment," The New Yorker, VI (March 8, 1930), 11.

"The Talk of the Town: Notes and Comment," The New Yorker, VI (March 15, 1930), 11-12.

"The Talk of the Town: Notes and Comment," The New Yorker, VI (March 22, 1930), 13.

"The Talk of the Town: Bulgakov," The New Yorker, VI (March 22, 1930), 16.

"A Reporter at Large: Snakes' Supper," The New Yorker, VI (March 22, 1930), 41-48.

"The Talk of the Town: Notes and Comment," The New Yorker, VI (March 29, 1930), 11-12.

"The Talk of the Town: Notes and Comment," The New Yorker, VI (April 5, 1930), 11-12.

"The Talk of the Town: Notes and Comment," The New Yorker, VI (April 12, 1930), 17-18.

"The Talk of the Town: Notes and Comment," The New Yorker, VI (April 19, 1930), 11-12.

"The Talk of the Town: Notes and Comment," The New Yorker, VI (April 26, 1930), 11.

"The Talk of the Town: Notes and Comment," The New Yorker, VI (May 3, 1930), 11-12.

"Barge Life on a Root Canal," The New Yorker, VI (May 3, 1930), 17.

"The Talk of the Town: Notes and Comment," The New Yorker, VI (May 10, 1930), 15-16.

"The Talk of the Town: Motorless Flight," The New Yorker, VI (May 10, 1930), 16.

"The Talk of the Town: Beauty in Light," The New Yorker, VI (May 10, 1930), 18.

"The Talk of the Town: Notes and Comment," The New Yorker, VI (May 17, 1930), 17-18.

"The Talk of the Town: Old Algiers," The New Yorker, VI (May 17, 1930), 20.

"The Talk of the Town: Notes and Comment," The New Yorker, VI (May 24, 1930), 11.

"Quo Vadimus?" The New Yorker, VI (May 24, 1930), 17-18.

"The Talk of the Town: Notes and Comment," The New Yorker, VI (May 31, 1930), 11-12.

"Slow Freights," The New Yorker, VI (May 31, 1930), 23.

"The Talk of the Town: Notes and Comment," The New Yorker, VI (June 7, 1930), 9-10.

"The Talk of the Town: Notes and Comment," The New Yorker, VI (June 14, 1930), 9-10.

"The Talk of the Town: Notes and Comment," The New Yorker, VI (June 21, 1930), 9-10.

"The Talk of the Town: Notes and Comment," The New Yorker, VI (June 28, 1930), 7-8.

"Presenting the Belmont Bar," The New Yorker, VI (June 28, 1930), 23.

"The Talk of the Town: Notes and Comment," The New Yorker, VI (July 5, 1930), 9-10.

"The Talk of the Town: Notes and Comment," The New Yorker, VI (July 12, 1930), 9-10.

"The Talk of the Town: Notes and Comment," The New Yorker, VI (July 19, 1930), 9-10.

"The Talk of the Town: Notes and Comment," The New Yorker, VI (July 26, 1930), 7-8.

"The Talk of the Town: De Mille on the Flossy," The New Yorker, VI (July 26, 1930), 9.

"The Talk of the Town: Notes and Comment," The New Yorker, VI (August 2, 1930), 7.

"The Talk of the Town: Notes and Comment," The New Yorker, VI (August 9, 1930), 7-8.

"The Talk of the Town: Notes and Comment," The New Yorker, VI (August 16, 1930), 9-10.

"The Talk of the Town: Notes and Comment," The New Yorker, VI (August 23, 1939), 7-8.

"Our Disillusioned Readers," The New Yorker, VI (August 23, 1930), 60-61. (Signed "Duncan Borg.")

"The Talk of the Town: Notes and Comment," The New Yorker, VI (August 30, 1930), 9-10.

"The Talk of the Town: Notes and Comment," The New Yorker, VI (September 6, 1930), 11-12.

"How to Make a Cat Trap," The New Yorker, VI (September 13, 1930), 26.

"The Talk of the Town: Notes and Comment," The New Yorker, VI (September 27, 1930), 17-18.

"The Talk of the Town: Notes and Comment," The New Yorker, VI (October 4, 1930), 17-18.

"The Other Side of the Case," The New Yorker, VI (October 4, 1930), 94-95. (Signed "C. S. Jones.")

"The Talk of the Town: Notes and Comment," The New Yorker, VI (October 11, 1930), 17-18.

"The Talk of the Town: Notes and Comment," The New Yorker, VI (October 18, 1930), 17-18.

"The Talk of the Town: Danbury Fair," The New Yorker, VI (October 18, 1930), 20.

"The Talk of the Town: Notes and Comment," The New Yorker, VI (October 25, 1930), 17-18.

"The Talk of the Town: Notes and Comment," The New Yorker, VI (November 1, 1930), 9-10.

"The Talk of the Town: Notes and Comment," The New Yorker, VI (November 8, 1930), 17-18.

"The Talk of the Town: Morning Worship," The New Yorker, VI (November 8, 1930), 21.

"How to Tell a Major Poet from a Minor Poet," The New Yorker, VI (November 8, 1930), 23-24.

"The Talk of the Town: Notes and Comment," The New Yorker, VI (November 15, 1930), 17-18.

"Voices," The New Yorker, VI (November 15, 1930), 32.

"The Talk of the Town: Notes and Comment," The New Yorker, VI (November 22, 1930), 17-18.

"The Talk of the Town: Notes and Comment," The New Yorker, VI (November 29, 1930), 17-18.

"The Talk of the Town: Notes and Comment," The New Yorker, VI (December 6, 1930), 19-20.

"The Talk of the Town: Notes and Comment," The New Yorker, VI (December 13, 1930), 17-18.

"The Talk of the Town: Bones," The New Yorker, VI (December 13, 1930), 20.

"The Talk of the Town: Fount," The New Yorker, VI (December 13, 1930), 21.

"The Talk of the Town: Notes and Comment," The New Yorker, VI (December 20, 1930), 13-14.

"Eeny Meeny Miny Mo," The New Yorker, VI (December 20, 1930), 21-22.

"The Talk of the Town: Notes and Comment," The New Yorker, VI (December 27, 1930), 9-10.

"The Talk of the Town: Milk and Water," The New Yorker, VI (December 27, 1930), 12.

1931

"Dr. Vinton," The Adelphi, I (January, 1931), 301-308. Also appears in Golden Book Magazine, XVI (October 1932), 353-357.

"The Talk of the Town: Notes and Comment," The New Yorker, VI (January 3, 1931), 9.

"The Talk of the Town: Notes and Comment," The New Yorker, VI (January 10, 1931), 9.

"Interview with Daisy," The New Yorker, VI (January 10, 1931), 20-21.

"Answer to Long Letters Department," The New Yorker, VI (January 10, 1931), 39-40. (Signed "Eustace Tilley.")

"The Talk of the Town: Notes and Comment," The New Yorker, VI (January 17, 1931), 13-14.

"The Talk of the Town: Notes and Comment," The New Yorker, VI (January 24, 1931), 9-10.

"The Talk of the Town: Spade-Calling," The New Yorker, VI (January 24, 1931), 10.

"The Talk of the Town: Notes and Comment," The New Yorker, VI (January 31, 1931), 9-10.

"The Talk of the Town: Notes and Comment," The New Yorker, VI (February 7, 1931), 9-10.

"The Talk of the Town: Notes and Comment," The New Yorker, VI (February 14, 1931), 11-12.

"The Talk of the Town: Gag," The New Yorker, VI (February 14, 1931), 12.

"The Talk of the Town: Notes and Comment," The New Yorker, VII (February 21, 1931), 9-10.

"The Talk of the Town: Trivia," The New Yorker, VII (February 21, 1931), 10.

"The Talk of the Town: Mr. Maloney's Ginsberg," The New Yorker, VII (February 21, 1931), 11.

"The Near-Demise of Mrs. Coe," The New Yorker, VII (February 21, 1931), 15-16.

"The Talk of the Town: Notes and Comment," The New Yorker, VII (February 28, 1931), 9-10.

"The Talk of the Town: F. A. O.," The New Yorker, VII (February 28, 1931), 11.

"The Talk of the Town: Notes and Comment," The New Yorker, VII (March 7, 1931), 17-18.

"The Talk of the Town: Notes and Comment," The New Yorker, VII (March 14, 1931), 13-14.

"The Talk of the Town: Notes and Comment," The New Yorker, VII (March 21, 1931), 11-12.

"The Talk of the Town: Notes and Comment," The New Yorker, VII (March 28, 1931), 13-14.

"The Urgency of an Agency," The New Republic, LXVI (April 1, 1931), 180-181.

"The Talk of the Town: Notes and Comment," The New Yorker, VII (April 4, 1931), 15-16.

"Hunger," The New Yorker, VII (April 4, 1931), 21.

"The Talk of the Town: Notes and Comment," The New Yorker, VII (April 11, 1931), 13-14.

"The Talk of the Town: Notes and Comment," The New Yorker, VII (April 18, 1931), 11-12.

"Profiles: Little Monarch," The New Yorker, VII (April 18, 1931), 24-26. (Signed "Andrew A. Freeman.")

"The Talk of the Town: Notes and Comment," The New Yorker, VII (April 25, 1931), 11-12.

"The Talk of the Town: Getting It There," The New Yorker, VII (April 25, 1931), 13.

"The Talk of the Town: Notes and Comment," The New Yorker, VII (May 2, 1931), 11-12.

"The Talk of the Town: Outposts," The New Yorker, VII (May 2, 1931), 14.

"The Talk of the Town: Notes and Comment," The New Yorker, VII (May 9, 1931), 13-14.

"The Talk of the Town: Key Men," The New Yorker, VII (May 9, 1931), 15.

"The Talk of the Town: Notes and Comment," The New Yorker, VII (May 16, 1931), 11-12.

"The Talk of the Town: Notes and Comment," The New Yorker, VII (May 23, 1931), 9-10.

"A Reporter at Large: Flying Slow," The New Yorker, VII (May 23, 1931), 43-48.

"The Talk of the Town: Notes and Comment," The New Yorker, VII (May 30, 1931), 9-10.

"The Talk of the Town: Notes and Comment," The New Yorker, VII (June 6, 1931), 11-12.

"The Talk of the Town: Notes and Comment," The New Yorker, VII (June 13, 1931), 11-12.

"The Talk of the Town: Visit," The New Yorker, VII (June 13, 1931), 14.

"The Talk of the Town: Notes and Comment," The New Yorker, VII (June 20, 1931), 7-8.

"The Talk of the Town: Notes and Comment," The New Yorker, VII (June 27, 1931), 7-8.

"The Talk of the Town: Notes and Comment," *The New Yorker*, VII (July 4, 1931), 9-10.

"The Talk of the Town: Personal Ships," *The New Yorker*, VII (July 4, 1931), 13.

"The Talk of the Town: Notes and Comment," *The New Yorker*, VII (July 11, 1931), 9-10.

"The Talk of the Town: Notes and Comment," *The New Yorker*, VII (July 18, 1931), 7-8.

"The Talk of the Town: Notes and Comment," *The New Yorker*, VII (July 25, 1931), 7-8.

"The Talk of the Town: Notes and Comment," *The New Yorker*, VII (August 1, 1931), 7-8.

"The Talk of the Town: Notes and Comment," *The New Yorker*, VII (August 8, 1931), 7-8.

"The Talk of the Town: s'nospmohT," *The New Yorker*, VII (August 8, 1931), 9.

"The Wings of Orville," *The New Yorker*, VII (August 8, 1931), 13-14.*

"The Talk of the Town: Notes and Comment," *The New Yorker*, VII (August 22, 1931), 9-10.

"The Talk of the Town: Notes and Comment," *The New Yorker*, VII (August 29, 1931), 9-10.

"The Talk of the Town: Notes and Comment," *The New Yorker*, VII (September 5, 1931), 9-10.

"The Talk of the Town: Notes and Comment," *The New Yorker*, VII (September 12, 1931), 13-14.

"The Talk of the Town: Notes and Comment," *The New Yorker*, VII (September 19, 1931), 11-12.

"The Talk of the Town: Notes and Comment," *The New Yorker*, VII (September 26, 1931), 9-10.

"The Talk of the Town: Notes and Comment," *The New Yorker*, VII (October 3, 1931), 15-16.

"The Talk of the Town: Notes and Comment," The New Yorker, VII (October 10, 1931), 15.

"The Talk of the Town: Decoys," The New Yorker, VII (October 10, 1931), 18.

"The Talk of the Town: G. W. Bridge," The New Yorker, VII (October 10, 1931), 19.

"The Key of Life," The New Yorker, VII (October 10, 1931), 21-23.

"The Talk of the Town: Notes and Comment," The New Yorker, VII (October 17, 1931), 11.

"It's About Time Department," The New Yorker, VII (October 17, 1931), 26-27. (Subtitled: "Anthology of Hope, Compiled by those Incorrigible Optimists, the Editors of The New Yorker, Who for Two Years Have Felt the Almost Daily Inspiration of the Country's Leaders of Thought.")

"The Talk of the Town: Notes and Comment," The New Yorker, VII (October 24, 1931), 11-12.

"The Talk of the Town: Notes and Comment," The New Yorker, VII (October 31, 1931), 11-12.

"The Talk of the Town: Wonder," The New Yorker, VII (October 31, 1931), 15.

"The Talk of the Town: Notes and Comment," The New Yorker, VII (November 7, 1931), 11-12.

"The Talk of the Town: Notes and Comment," The New Yorker, VII (November 14, 1931), 11-12.

"The Talk of the Town: Notes and Comment," The New Yorker, VII (November 21, 1931), 11.

"The Talk of the Town: Notes and Comment," The New Yorker, VII (November 28, 1931), 11.

"The Talk of the Town: Carted Stag," The New Yorker, VII (November 28, 1931), 14.

"The Talk of the Town: Notes and Comment," The New Yorker, VII (December 5, 1931), 13-14.

"Hark! Hark! The Turncoats," The New Yorker, VII (December 5, 1931), 28.

"The Talk of the Town: Notes and Comment," The New Yorker, VII (December 12, 1931), 13.

"The Talk of the Town: Notes and Comment," The New Yorker, VII (December 19, 1931), 11-12.

"The Talk of the Town: Notes and Comment," The New Yorker, VII (December 26, 1931), 7.

"Washing Up," The New Yorker, VII (December 26, 1931), 17.

1932

"The Talk of the Town: Notes and Comment," The New Yorker, VII (January 2, 1932), 9-10.

"The Talk of the Town: Notes and Comment," The New Yorker, VII (January 9, 1932), 9-10.

"The Talk of the Town: Notes and Comment," The New Yorker, VII (January 16, 1932), 9-10.

"The Talk of the Town: Notes and Comment," The New Yorker, VII (January 23, 1932), 9-10.

"The Talk of the Town: After the Ball," The New Yorker, VII (January 23, 1932), 10.

"The Talk of the Town: Notes and Comment," The New Yorker, VII (January 30, 1932), 7-8.

"The Talk of the Town: Notes and Comment," The New Yorker, VII (February 6, 1932), 9.

"The Bishop Is Here," The New Yorker, VII (February 6, 1932), 17.

"The Talk of the Town: Notes and Comment," The New Yorker, VII (February 13, 1932), 7-8.

"The Man in 32," The New Yorker, VII (February 13, 1932), 18.

"The Talk of the Town: Notes and Comment," The New Yorker, VIII (February 20, 1932), 11.

"The Talk of the Town: Clique," The New Yorker, VIII (February 20, 1932), 13.

"A Reporter at Large: Midwinter Madness," The New Yorker, VIII (February 20, 1932), 38-44.*

"The Talk of the Town: Notes and Comment," The New Yorker, VIII (February 27, 1932), 7-8.

"The Talk of the Town: Notes and Comment," The New Yorker, VIII (March 5, 1932), 13-14.

"The Talk of the Town: Notes and Comment," The New Yorker, VIII (March 12, 1932), 9.

"Obituary," The New Yorker, VIII (March 12, 1932), 16.*

"The Talk of the Town: Notes and Comment," The New Yorker, VIII (March 19, 1932), 11-12.

"The Talk of the Town: Notes and Comment," The New Yorker, VIII (March 26, 1932), 9-10.

"The Talk of the Town: Notes and Comment," The New Yorker, VIII (April 2, 1932), 7.

"The Talk of the Town: Notes and Comment," The New Yorker, VIII (April 9, 1932), 9-10.

"The Talk of the Town: Notes and Comment," The New Yorker, VIII (April 16, 1932), 9-10.

"A Reporter at Large: Alma Mater's Eggs," The New Yorker, VIII (April 16, 1932), 36-42.*

"The Talk of the Town: Notes and Comment," The New Yorker, VIII (April 23, 1932), 9-10.

"Growing Up in New Canaan," The New Yorker, VIII (April 23, 1932), 15-16. (Signed "Gil Borg.")

"The Talk of the Town: Notes and Comment," The New Yorker, VIII (April 30, 1932), 9-10.

"The Talk of the Town: Notes and Comment," The New Yorker, VIII (May 7, 1932), 9-10.

"The Talk of the Town: Notes and Comment," The New Yorker, VIII (May 14, 1932), 9-10.

"A Reporter at Large: Four Miles over Timber," The New Yorker, VIII (May 14, 1932), 34-40. *

"The Talk of the Town: Notes and Comment," The New Yorker, VIII (May 21, 1932), 9-10.

"The Talk of the Town: Better Mousetraps," The New Yorker, VIII (May 21, 1932), 11.

"The Talk of the Town: Notes and Comment," The New Yorker, VIII (May 28, 1932), 9-10.

"The Talk of the Town: Notes and Comment," The New Yorker, VIII (June 4, 1932), 9-10.

"The Talk of the Town: Notes and Comment," The New Yorker, VIII (June 11, 1932), 7-8.

"The Talk of the Town: Notes and Comment," The New Yorker, VIII (June 18, 1932), 7-8.

"The Talk of the Town: Notes and Comment," The New Yorker, VIII (June 25, 1932), 7-8.

"The Talk of the Town: Notes and Comment," The New Yorker, VIII (July 2, 1932), 5-6.

"The Talk of the Town: Notes and Comment," The New Yorker, VIII (July 9, 1932), 7-8.

"The Talk of the Town: Notes and Comment," The New Yorker, VIII (July 15, 1932), 5-6.

"The Talk of the Town: Notes and Comment," The New Yorker, VIII (July 23, 1932), 5-6.

"Alice, Where Wert Thou?" The New Yorker, VIII (July 23, 1932), 16.

"The Talk of the Town: Notes and Comment," The New Yorker, VIII (July 30, 1932), 5-6.

"The Talk of the Town: Notes and Comment," The New Yorker, VIII (August 6, 1932), 7-8.

"Roosevelts: Just Roosevelts," The New Yorker, VIII (August 6, 1932), 18.

"The Talk of the Town: Notes and Comment," The New Yorker, VIII (August 13, 1932), 5-6.

"The Talk of the Town: Notes and Comment," The New Yorker, VIII (August 20, 1932), 7-8.

"The Talk of the Town: Notes and Comment," The New Yorker, VIII (September 3, 1932), 9-10.

"The Talk of the Town: Notes and Comment," The New Yorker, VIII (September 10, 1932), 9-10.

"The Talk of the Town: Notes and Comment," The New Yorker, VIII (September 17, 1932), 9-10.

"The Talk of the Town: Notes and Comment," The New Yorker, VIII (September 24, 1932), 9-10.

"The Talk of the Town: Notes and Comment," The New Yorker, VIII (October 1, 1932), 11-12.

"The Talk of the Town: Notes and Comment," The New Yorker, VIII (October 8, 1932), 9-10.

"The Talk of the Town: Notes and Comment," The New Yorker, VIII (October 15, 1932), 11-12.

"The Talk of the Town: Notes and Comment," The New Yorker, VIII (October 22, 1932), 9-10.

"The Talk of the Town: Notes and Comment," The New Yorker, VIII (October 29, 1932), 7-8.

"The Talk of the Town: Notes and Comment," The New Yorker, VIII (November 5, 1932), 13-14.

"The Talk of the Town: Notes and Comment," The New Yorker, VIII (November 12, 1932), 9-10.

"The Talk of the Town: Notes and Comment," The New Yorker, VIII (November 19, 1932), 9-10.

"The Landslide," The New Yorker, VIII (November 19, 1932), 21.

"The Talk of the Town: Notes and Comment," The New Yorker, VIII (November 26, 1932), 9-10.

"The Talk of the Town: Besichtigung," The New Yorker, VIII (November 26, 1932), 11.

"The Talk of the Town: Notes and Comment," The New Yorker, VIII (December 3, 1932), 11-12.

"The Talk of the Town: Notes and Comment," The New Yorker, VIII (December 10, 1932), 11-12.

"The Talk of the Town: Notes and Comment," The New Yorker, VIII (December 17, 1932), 9-10.

"The Talk of the Town: Notes and Comment," The New Yorker, VIII (December 24, 1932), 7-8.

"The Talk of the Town: Notes and Comment," The New Yorker, VIII (December 31, 1932), 5-6.

1933

"The Talk of the Town: Notes and Comment," The New Yorker, VIII (January 7, 1933), 9-10.

"Swing Low, Sweet Upswing," The New Yorker, VIII (January 7, 1933), 14.

"The Talk of the Town: Notes and Comment," The New Yorker, VIII (January 14, 1933), 9-10.

"The Talk of the Town: Adjustment," The New Yorker, VIII (January 14, 1933), 10.

"The Talk of the Town: Notes and Comment," The New Yorker, VIII (January 21, 1933), 9-10.

"The Talk of the Town: Notes and Comment," The New Yorker, VIII (January 28, 1933), 7-8.

"The Talk of the Town: Jiu-Jitsu," The New Yorker, VIII (January 28, 1933), 8.

"The Motor Boat Show," The New Yorker, VIII (January 28, 1933), 45-46. (Signed "V-23.")

"The Talk of the Town: Notes and Comment," The New Yorker, VIII (February 4, 1933), 7-8.

"The Talk of the Town: Notes and Comment," The New Yorker, VIII (February 11, 1933), 9-10.

"The Talk of the Town: Notes and Comment," The New Yorker, IX (February 18, 1933), 9-10.

"Journey's Dead-End," The New Yorker, IX (February 18, 1933), 15-16.

"The Talk of the Town: Notes and Comment," The New Yorker, IX (February 25, 1933), 11-12.

"The Talk of the Town: Notes and Comment," The New Yorker, IX (March 4, 1933), 9-10.

"The Talk of the Town: Notes and Comment," The New Yorker, IX (March 11, 1933), 9-10.

"The Talk of the Town: Notes and Comment," The New Yorker, IX (March 18, 1933), 7.

"The Talk of the Town: Notes and Comment," The New Yorker, IX (March 25, 1933), 7-8.

"The Talk of the Town: Notes and Comment," The New Yorker, IX (April 1, 1933), 7-8.

"The Talk of the Town: Notes and Comment," The New Yorker, IX (April 8, 1933), 13-14.

"The Talk of the Town: Notes and Comment," The New Yorker, IX (April 15, 1933), 7-8.

"The Talk of the Town: Notes and Comment," The New Yorker, IX (April 22, 1933), 7-8.

"The Talk of the Town: Notes and Comment," The New Yorker, IX (April 29, 1933), 9-10.

"The Talk of the Town: Pour le Sport," The New Yorker, IX (April 29, 1933), 13.

"The Talk of the Town: Notes and Comment," The New Yorker, IX (May 6, 1933), 11-12.

"Alice Through the Cellophane: I. Down the Rabbit Hole," The New Yorker, IX (May 6, 1933), 18-20.

"The Talk of the Town: Notes and Comment," The New Yorker, IX (May 13, 1933), 9-10.

"The Talk of the Town: Mall Life," The New Yorker, IX (May 13, 1933), 13.

"Alice Through the Cellophane: II. The Pool of Tears," The New Yorker, IX (May 13, 1933), 16-17.

"The Talk of the Town: Notes and Comment," The New Yorker, IX (May 20, 1933), 9-10.

"Alice Through the Cellophane: III. Advice from a Caterpillar," The New Yorker, IX (May 20, 1933), 17-18.

"The Talk of the Town: Notes and Comment," The New Yorker, IX (May 27, 1933), 7-8.

"The Talk of the Town: Notes and Comment," The New Yorker, IX (June 3, 1933), 7-8.

"The Talk of the Town: Notes and Comment," The New Yorker, IX (June 10, 1933), 7-8.

"A Study of the Clinical 'We'," The New Yorker, IX (June 10, 1933), 13.

"The Talk of the Town: Notes and Comment," The New Yorker, IX (June 17, 1933), 5-6.

"The Talk of the Town: Notes and Comment," The New Yorker, IX (June 24, 1933), 7-8.

"The Talk of the Town: Notes and Comment," The New Yorker, IX (July 1, 1933), 7-8.

"The Talk of the Town: Notes and Comment," The New Yorker, IX (July 8, 1933), 5.

"The Talk of the Town: Notes and Comment," The New Yorker, IX (July 15, 1933), 5.

"Old Roads of Long Island," The New Yorker, IX (July 15, 1933), 20.

"The Talk of the Town: Notes and Comment," The New Yorker, IX (July 22, 1933), 7-8.

"The Talk of the Town: Beginnings," The New Yorker, IX (July 22, 1933), 8.

"The Talk of the Town: Notes and Comment," The New Yorker, IX (July 29, 1933), 5-6.

"The Talk of the Town: Notes and Comment," The New Yorker, IX (August 5, 1933), 5-6.

"The Talk of the Town: Notes and Comment," The New Yorker, IX (August 12, 1933), 5.

"The Talk of the Town: Notes and Comment," The New Yorker, IX (August 19, 1933), 7-8.

"The Talk of the Town: Notes and Comment," The New Yorker, IX (August 26, 1933), 7.

"The Talk of the Town: Notes and Comment," The New Yorker, IX (September 2, 1933), 5.

"The Talk of the Town: Notes and Comment," The New Yorker, IX (September 9, 1933), 9.

"The Talk of the Town: Notes and Comment," The New Yorker, IX (September 16, 1933), 11-12.

"The Talk of the Town: Notes and Comment," The New Yorker, IX (September 23, 1933), 9-10.

"The Talk of the Town: Notes and Comment," The New Yorker, IX (September 30, 1933), 9-10.

"The Talk of the Town: Notes and Comment," The New Yorker, IX (October 7, 1933), 11-12.

"The Talk of the Town: Notes and Comment," The New Yorker, IX (October 14, 1933), 13-14.

"The Crack of Doom," The New Yorker, IX (October 14, 1933), 19-20.

"The Talk of the Town: Notes and Comment," The New Yorker, IX (October 21, 1933), 15-16.

"The Talk of the Town: Notes and Comment," The New Yorker, IX (October 28, 1933), 9.

"A Reporter at Large: News Outside the Door," The New Yorker, IX (October 28, 1933), 54-60. (Signed "E. Bagworm Wren.")

"The Talk of the Town: Notes and Comment," The New Yorker, IX (November 4, 1933), 9-10.

"The Talk of the Town: Notes and Comment," The New Yorker, IX (November 11, 1933), 13-14.

"The Talk of the Town: Notes and Comment," The New Yorker, IX (November 18, 1933), 15-16.

"The Talk of the Town: Notes and Comment," The New Yorker, IX (November 25, 1933), 13-14.

"The Supremacy of Uruguay," The New Yorker, IX (November 25, 1933), 18-19.

"The Talk of the Town: Notes and Comment," The New Yorker, IX (December 2, 1933), 11-12.

"The Talk of the Town: Notes and Comment," The New Yorker, IX (December 9, 1933), 17.

"The Talk of the Town: Then and Now," The New Yorker, IX (December 9, 1933), 18.

"The Talk of the Town: Notes and Comment," The New Yorker, IX (December 16, 1933), 11-12.

"The Talk of the Town: Notes and Comment," The New Yorker, IX (December 23, 1933), 7-8.

"The Talk of the Town: Notes and Comment," The New Yorker, IX (December 30, 1933), 7-8.

1934

"The Talk of the Town: Notes and Comment," The New Yorker, IX (January 6, 1934), 15-16.

"The Talk of the Town: Notes and Comment," The New Yorker, IX (January 13, 1934), 11-12.

"The Talk of the Town: Notes and Comment," The New Yorker, IX (January 20, 1934), 5-6.

"The Talk of the Town: Notes and Comment," The New Yorker, IX (January 27, 1934), 11-12.

"Dusk in Fierce Pajamas," The New Yorker, IX (January 27, 1934), 16-17.

"The Talk of the Town: Notes and Comment," The New Yorker, IX (February 3, 1934), 11-12.

"The Talk of the Town: Notes and Comment," The New Yorker, IX (February 10, 1934), 11-12.

"The Talk of the Town: Many Happy Returns," The New Yorker, IX (February 10, 1934), 12.

"The Talk of the Town: Notes and Comment," The New Yorker, X (February 17, 1934), 11-14.

"The Talk of the Town: Fair Play," The New Yorker, X (February 17, 1934), 14.

"The Talk of the Town: Notes and Comment," The New Yorker, X (February 24, 1934), 11-12.

"The Talk of the Town: Notes and Comment," The New Yorker, X (March 3, 1934), 13-14.

"The Talk of the Town: Notes and Comment," The New Yorker, X (March 10, 1934), 11-12.

"The Talk of the Town: Notes and Comment," The New Yorker, X (March 17, 1934), 15-16.

"The Talk of the Town: Notes and Comment," The New Yorker, X (March 24, 1934), 11-12.

"The Talk of the Town: Notes and Comment," The New Yorker, X (March 31, 1934), 11-12.

"The Talk of the Town: Notes and Comment," The New Yorker, X (April 7, 1934), 17-18.

"Fin de Saison--Palm Beach," The New Yorker, X (April 7, 1934), 24-25.

"The Talk of the Town: Notes and Comment," The New Yorker, X (April 14, 1934), 15-16.

"The Talk of the Town: Notes and Comment," The New Yorker, X (April 21, 1934), 11-12.

"The Talk of the Town: Notes and Comment," The New Yorker, X (April 28, 1934), 13-14.

"The Talk of the Town: Notes and Comment," The New Yorker, X (May 5, 1934), 15-16.

"The Talk of the Town: Zephyr," The New Yorker, X (May 5, 1934), 19.

"The Talk of the Town: Notes and Comment," The New Yorker, X (May 12, 1934), 13-14.

"The Talk of the Town: Notes and Comment," The New Yorker, X (May 19, 1934), 13-14.

"The Talk of the Town: Notes and Comment," The New Yorker, X (May 26, 1934), 13-14.

"Onward and Upward with the Arts: The Literary Business," The New Yorker, X (May 26, 1934), 39-46.

"The Talk of the Town: Notes and Comment," The New Yorker, X (June 2, 1934), 11-12.

"The Talk of the Town: Notes and Comment," The New Yorker, X (June 9, 1934), 9-10.

"The Talk of the Town: Middle Class," The New Yorker, X (June 9, 1934), 14.

"The Talk of the Town: Notes and Comment," The New Yorker, X (June 16, 1934), 9-10.

"My Man," The New Yorker, X (June 16, 1934), 15. (Signed "Squire Cuthbert.")

"The Talk of the Town: Notes and Comment," The New Yorker, X (June 23, 1934), 9-10.

"The Talk of the Town: Notes and Comment," The New Yorker, X (June 30, 1934), 9-10.

"As the Oith Toins," Harper's Magazine, CLXIX (July, 1934), 251-252.

"The Talk of the Town: Notes and Comment," The New Yorker, X (July 7, 1934), 9-10.

"The Talk of the Town: Notes and Comment," The New Yorker, X (July 14, 1934), 9-10.

"The Talk of the Town: Notes and Comment," The New Yorker, X (July 21, 1934), 9-10.

"The Talk of the Town: Notes and Comment," The New Yorker, X (July 28, 1934), 9-10.

"The Talk of the Town: Notes and Comment," The New Yorker, X (August 4, 1934), 9-10.

"The Talk of the Town: Notes and Comment," The New Yorker, X (August 11, 1934), 7-8.

"The Special Luncheon," The New Yorker, X (August 11, 1934), 23-24.

"The Talk of the Town: Notes and Comment," The New Yorker, X (August 18, 1934), 7-8.

"The Talk of the Town: Notes and Comment," The New Yorker, X (August 25, 1934), 11-12.

"The Talk of the Town: Notes and Comment," The New Yorker, X (September 1, 1934), 11-12.

"The Talk of the Town: Chatterboxes," The New Yorker, X (September 1, 1934), 13.

"A Century of Progress," The New Yorker, X (September 1, 1934), 18-19.

"The Talk of the Town: Notes and Comment," The New Yorker, X (September 8, 1934), 17-18.

"The Talk of the Town: Notes and Comment," The New Yorker, X (September 15, 1934), 21-22.

"The Talk of the Town: Notes and Comment," The New Yorker, X (September 22, 1934), 15-16.

"Ear Pictures," The New Yorker, X (September 22, 1934), 24-25.

"The Talk of the Town: Notes and Comment," The New Yorker, X (September 29, 1934), 9-10.

"A Reporter at Sea," The New Yorker, X (September 29, 1934), 37-38.

"The Talk of the Town: Notes and Comment," The New Yorker, X (October 6, 1934), 15-16.

"The Talk of the Town: Notes and Comment," The New Yorker, X (October 13, 1934), 15-16.

"The Talk of the Town: Notes and Comment," The New Yorker, X (October 20, 1934), 11-12.

"The Talk of the Town: Notes and Comment," The New Yorker, X (October 27, 1934), 11.

"The Talk of the Town: Notes and Comment," The New Yorker, X (November 3, 1934), 13-14.

"The Talk of the Town: Notes and Comment," The New Yorker, X (November 10, 1934), 13-14.

"Our Tardy Readers," The New Yorker, X (November 10, 1934), 84-86. (Signed "The Editors.")

"The Talk of the Town: Notes and Comment," The New Yorker, X (November 17, 1934), 13-14.

"The Talk of the Town: Notes and Comment," The New Yorker, X (November 24, 1934), 11-12.

"The Talk of the Town: Notes and Comment," The New Yorker, X (December 1, 1934), 17-18.

"The Talk of the Town: Notes and Comment," The New Yorker, X (December 8, 1934), 17-18.

"Onward and Upward with the Arts: St. Nicholas League," The New Yorker, X (December 8, 1934), 38-52.

"The Talk of the Town: Notes and Comment," The New Yorker, X (December 15, 1934), 17-18.

"The Talk of the Town: Magic," The New Yorker, X (December 15, 1934), 18.

"The Talk of the Town: Notes and Comment," The New Yorker, X (December 22, 1934), 7-8.

"The Talk of the Town: Notes and Comment," The New Yorker, X (December 29, 1934), 9-10.

1935

"The Talk of the Town: Notes and Comment," The New Yorker, X (January 5, 1935), 13-14.

"The Talk of the Town: Notes and Comment," The New Yorker, X (January 12, 1935), 11-12.

"The Talk of the Town: Notes and Comment," The New Yorker, X (January 19, 1935), 9-10.

"The Talk of the Town: Notes and Comment," The New Yorker, X (January 26, 1935), 11-12.

"The Motor Boat Show," The New Yorker, X (January 26, 1935), 47-48.

"The Talk of the Town: Notes and Comment," The New Yorker, X (February 2, 1935), 11-12.

"The Street of the Dead," The New Yorker, X (February 2, 1935), 16.* (Signed "Elliott Senior.")

"The Talk of the Town: Notes and Comment," The New Yorker, X (February 9, 1935), 13-14.

"The Talk of the Town: Notes and Comment," The New Yorker, XI (February 16, 1935), 11-12.

"Out of Town: Snow Train," The New Yorker, XI (February 16, 1935), 32-42.

"The Talk of the Town: Notes and Comment," The New Yorker, XI (February 23, 1935), 7-8.

"The Talk of the Town: Notes and Comment," The New Yorker, XI (March 2, 1935), 9-10.

"The Talk of the Town: Notes and Comment," The New Yorker, XI (March 9, 1935), 9-10.

"The Talk of the Town: Notes and Comment," The New Yorker, XI (March 16, 1935), 17-18.

"The Talk of the Town: Notes and Comment," The New Yorker, XI (March 23, 1935), 9-10.

"The Talk of the Town: Straight Up," The New Yorker, XI (March 23, 1935), 11.

"The Dove's Nest," The New Yorker, XI (March 23, 1935), 15.*

"The Talk of the Town: Notes and Comment," The New Yorker, XI (March 30, 1935), 11-12.

"The Talk of the Town: Notes and Comment," The New Yorker, XI (April 6, 1935), 13-14.

"The Talk of the Town: Notes and Comment," The New Yorker, XI (April 13, 1935), 15-16.

"The Talk of the Town: Notes and Comment," The New Yorker, XI (April 20, 1935), 11-12.

"Onward and Upward with the Arts: Terse Verse," The New Yorker, XI (April 20, 1935), 32-38.*

"The Talk of the Town: Notes and Comment," The New Yorker, XI (April 27, 1935), 11-12.

"The Talk of the Town: Spells," The New Yorker, XI (April 27, 1935), 13.

"The Talk of the Town: Notes and Comment," The New Yorker, XI (May 4, 1935), 9-10.

"The Talk of the Town: Notes and Comment," The New Yorker, XI (May 11, 1935), 17-18.

"The Talk of the Town: Bird Walk," The New Yorker, XI (May 11, 1935), 18.

"The Talk of the Town: Notes and Comment," The New Yorker, XI (May 18, 1935), 13-14.

"The Talk of the Town: Notes and Comment," The New Yorker, XI (May 25, 1935), 11-12.

"The Talk of the Town: Notes and Comment," The New Yorker, XI (June 1, 1935), 9-10.

"The Talk of the Town: Notes and Comment," The New Yorker, XI (June 8, 1935), 11-12.

"The Talk of the Town: Notes and Comment," The New Yorker, XI (June 15, 1935), 7-8.

"The Talk of the Town: Notes and Comment," The New Yorker, XI (June 22, 1935), 7-8.

"The Talk of the Town: Notes and Comment," The New Yorker, XI (June 29, 1935), 9-10.

"Lady Before Breakfast," The American Mercury, XXXV (July, 1935), 285.

"The Talk of the Town: Notes and Comment," The New Yorker, XI (July 6, 1935), 7-8.

"The Talk of the Town: Notes and Comment," The New Yorker, XI (July 13, 1935), 7-8.

"The Talk of the Town: Notes and Comment," The New Yorker, XI (July 20, 1935), 7-8.

"The Talk of the Town: Notes and Comment," The New Yorker, XI (July 27, 1935), 9-10.

"The Talk of the Town: Notes and Comment," The New Yorker, XI (August 3, 1935), 7-8.

"Much Ado about Plenty," The New Yorker, XI (August 3, 1935), 23-24.

"The Talk of the Town: Notes and Comment," The New Yorker, XI (August 10, 1935), 7-8.

"The Talk of the Town: Notes and Comment," The New Yorker, XI (August 17, 1935), 7-8.

"The Talk of the Town: Notes and Comment," The New Yorker, XI (August 24, 1935), 11-12.

"The Talk of the Town: Notes and Comment," The New Yorker, XI (August 31, 1935), 9-10.

"The Talk of the Town: Notes and Comment," The New Yorker, XI (September 7, 1935), 15-16.

"The Talk of the Town: Notes and Comment," The New Yorker, XI (September 14, 1935), 13-14.

"The Talk of the Town: Notes and Comment," The New Yorker, XI (October 5, 1935), 17-18.

"The Talk of the Town: Notes and Comment," The New Yorker, XI (October 12, 1935), 13-14.

"The Talk of the Town: Notes and Comment," The New Yorker, XI (October 19, 1935), 15-16.

"The Talk of the Town: Notes and Comment," The New Yorker, XI (October 26, 1935), 15-16.

"The Talk of the Town: Notes and Comment," The New Yorker, XI (November 2, 1935), 13-14.

"The Talk of the Town: Notes and Comment," The New Yorker, XI (November 9, 1935), 11-12.

"The Talk of the Town: Notes and Comment," The New Yorker, XI (November 16, 1935), 13-14.

"The Talk of the Town: Notes and Comment," The New Yorker, XI (November 23, 1935), 9-10.

"The Talk of the Town: Notes and Comment," The New Yorker, XI (November 30, 1935), 11-12.

'Irtnog," The New Yorker, XI (November 30, 1935), 17-18.*

"The Talk of the Town: Notes and Comment," The New Yorker, XI (December 7, 1935), 27-28.

"Getting Along with Women," The New Yorker, XI (December 7, 1935), 35-36.*

"The Talk of the Town: Notes and Comment," The New Yorker, XI (December 14, 1935), 19-20.

"The Talk of the Town: Notes and Comment," The New Yorker, XI (December 21, 1935), 11-12.

"The Talk of the Town: Notes and Comment," The New Yorker, XI (December 28, 1935), 9-10.

1936

"The Talk of the Town: Notes and Comment," The New Yorker, XI (January 4, 1936), 9-10.

"The Talk of the Town: Notes and Comment," The New Yorker, XI (January 11, 1936), 9-10.

"The Talk of the Town: Clarence Day," The New Yorker, XI (January 11, 1936), 10.

"The Talk of the Town: Notes and Comment," The New Yorker, XI (January 18, 1936), 7.

"The Talk of the Town: Notes and Comment," The New Yorker, XI (January 25, 1936), 9-10.

"Onward and Upward with the Arts: A Blessed Event--I," The New Yorker, XI (January 25, 1936), 29-36.*

"The Talk of the Town: Notes and Comment," The New Yorker, XI (February 1, 1936), 11-12.

"Onward and Upward with the Arts: A Blessed Event--II," The New Yorker, XI (February 1, 1936), 31-35.*

"The Talk of the Town: Notes and Comment," The New Yorker, XI (February 8, 1936), 11-12.

"The Talk of the Town: Notes and Comment," The New Yorker, XI (February 15, 1936), 11-12.

"The Talk of the Town: Notes and Comment," The New Yorker, XII (February 22, 1936), 9-10.

"The Talk of the Town: Notes and Comment," The New Yorker, XII (February 29, 1936), 9-10.

"The Talk of the Town: Notes and Comment," The New Yorker, XII (March 7, 1936), 15-16.

"The Talk of the Town: Notes and Comment," The New Yorker, XII (March 14, 1936), 11-12.

"A Guide to the Pronunciation of Words in 'Time'," The New Yorker, XII (March 14, 1936), 16.*

"The Talk of the Town: Notes and Comment," The New Yorker, XII (March 21, 1936), 11-12.

"The Talk of the Town: Notes and Comment," The New Yorker, XII (March 28, 1936), 15-16.

"The Talk of the Town: Notes and Comment," The New Yorker, XII (April 4, 1936), 15-16.

"The Talk of the Town: Notes and Comment," The New Yorker, XII (April 11, 1936) 9-10.

"The Talk of the Town: Greek Games," The New Yorker, XII (April 11, 1936), 10.

"The Talk of the Town: Notes and Comment," The New Yorker, XII (April 18, 1936), 11-12.

"The Talk of the Town: Pulse-Quickening," The New Yorker, XII (April 18, 1936), 12.

"The Talk of the Town: Notes and Comment," The New Yorker, XII (April 25, 1936), 9-10.

"The Talk of the Town: Notes and Comment," The New Yorker, XII (May 2, 1936), 11-12.

"H. L. Mencken Meets a Poet in the West Side Y.M.C.A.," The Saturday Review of Literature, XIV (May 9, 1936), 10-11.

"The Talk of the Town: Notes and Comment," The New Yorker, XII (May 9, 1936), 13-14.

"The Talk of the Town: Notes and Comment," The New Yorker, XII (May 16, 1936), 11-12.

"Onward and Upward with the Arts: Farewell, My Lovely!"

The New Yorker, XII (May 16, 1936), 20-22.* (Signed "Lee Strout White.")

"Marble-Top," Scholastic, XXVIII (May 23, 1936), 9.

"The Talk of the Town: Notes and Comment," The New Yorker, XII (May 23, 1936), 11-12.

"The Talk of the Town: Notes and Comment," The New Yorker, XII (May 30, 1936), 9-10.

"The Talk of the Town: Village Gardens," The New Yorker, XII (May 30, 1936), 10.

"The Talk of the Town: Notes and Comment," The New Yorker, XII (June 6, 1936), 7-8.

"The Talk of the Town: Notes and Comment," The New Yorker, XII (June 13, 1936), 9-10.

"The Talk of the Town: Notes and Comment," The New Yorker, XII (June 20, 1936), 9-10.

"The Talk of the Town: Notes and Comment," The New Yorker, XII (June 27, 1936), 9-10.

"The Talk of the Town: Under the Lindens," The New Yorker, XII (June 27, 1936), 10.

"The Talk of the Town: Notes and Comment," The New Yorker, XII (July 4, 1936), 7-8.

"The Talk of the Town: Notes and Comment," The New Yorker, XII (July 11, 1936), 7-8.

"The Talk of the Town: Notes and Comment," The New Yorker, XII (July 18, 1936), 7-8.

"The Talk of the Town: Notes and Comment," The New Yorker, XII (July 25, 1936), 9-10.

"The Talk of the Town: Notes and Comment," The New Yorker, XII (August 1, 1936), 7-8.

"The Talk of the Town: Notes and Comment," The New Yorker, XII (August 8, 1936), 7-8.

"The Talk of the Town: Notes and Comment," The New Yorker, XII (August 15, 1936), 9-10.

"The Talk of the Town: Notes and Comment," The New Yorker, XII (August 22, 1936), 9-10.

"The Talk of the Town: Pooch Palace," The New Yorker, XII (August 22, 1936), 11.

"The Talk of the Town: Notes and Comment," The New Yorker, XII (August 29, 1936), 7-8.

"The Talk of the Town: Notes and Comment," The New Yorker, XII (September 5, 1936), 9-10.

"The Talk of the Town: Tourist-Camps," The New Yorker, XII (September 5, 1936), 12.

"The Talk of the Town: Notes and Comment," The New Yorker, XII (September 26, 1936), 7-8.

"The Talk of the Town: Notes and Comment," The New Yorker, XII (October 3, 1936), 9-10.

"You Can't Resettle Me! A Defense of New York City by a Stubborn Inhabitant." The Saturday Evening Post, CCIX (October 10, 1936), 8-9, 91-92.

"The Talk of the Town: Notes and Comment," The New Yorker, XII (October 10, 1936), 13-14.

"The Talk of the Town: Notes and Comment," The New Yorker, XII (October 17, 1936), 13-14.

"The Talk of the Town: Notes and Comment," The New Yorker, XII (October 24, 1936), 9-10.

"The Talk of the Town: Notes and Comment," The New Yorker, XII (October 31, 1936), 9-10.

"The Talk of the Town: Notes and Comment," The New Yorker, XII (November 7, 1936), 11-12.

"The Talk of the Town: Notes and Comment," The New Yorker, XII (November 14, 1936), 21-22.

"The Talk of the Town: Around the Corner," The New Yorker, XII (November 14, 1936), 27.

"The Talk of the Town: Notes and Comment," The New Yorker, XII (November 21, 1936), 11-12.

"The Talk of the Town: Notes and Comment," The New Yorker, XII (November 28, 1936), 9-10.

"The Talk of the Town: Notes and Comment," The New Yorker, XII (December 5, 1936), 17-18.

"The Talk of the Town: Notes and Comment," The New Yorker, XII (December 12, 1936), 17-18.

"The Talk of the Town: Trees," The New Yorker, XII (December 12, 1936), 18.

"The Talk of the Town: Notes and Comment," The New Yorker, XII (December 19, 1936), 11-12.

"The Talk of the Town: Molasses in January," The New Yorker, XII (December 19, 1936), 19.

"Open-Letters Department," The New Yorker, XII (December 19, 1936), 64. (Signed "Eustace Tilley.")

"The Talk of the Town: Notes and Comment," The New Yorker, XII (December 26, 1936), 7-8.

1937

"The Talk of the Town: Notes and Comment," The New Yorker, XII (January 2, 1937), 9-10.

"The Talk of the Town: Notes and Comment," The New Yorker, XII (January 9, 1937), 11-12.

"The Talk of the Town: Notes and Comment," The New Yorker, XII (January 16, 1937), 9-10.

"The Talk of the Town: Ice Pond," The New Yorker, XII (January 16, 1937), 10.

"The Talk of the Town: Notes and Comment," The New Yorker, XII (January 23, 1937), 9-10.

"The Talk of the Town: Notes and Comment," The New Yorker, XII (January 30, 1937), 9-10.

"'The Readers' Digest Discovers the Bible,'" The New Yorker, XII (January 30, 1937), 20.

"The Talk of the Town: Notes and Comment," The New Yorker, XII (February 6, 1937), 9-10.

"The Talk of the Town: Notes and Comment," The New Yorker, XII (February 13, 1937), 9-10.

"The Talk of the Town: Notes and Comment," The New Yorker, XIII (February 20, 1937), 9-10.

"The Talk of the Town: Notes and Comment," The New Yorker, XIII (February 27, 1937), 11-12.

"The Talk of the Town: The Great Indoors," The New Yorker, XIII (February 27, 1937), 12.

"The Talk of the Town: Notes and Comment," The New Yorker, XIII (March 6, 1937), 13-14.

"Department of Correction, Amplification, and Abuse," The New Yorker, XIII (March 6, 1937), 46-50. (Signed "P. B. Publico.")

"The Talk of the Town: Notes and Comment," The New Yorker, XIII (March 13, 1937), 11-12.

"The Talk of the Town: Notes and Comment," The New Yorker, XIII (March 20, 1937), 15-16.

"The Talk of the Town: Notes and Comment," The New Yorker, XIII (March 27, 1937), 9-10.

"The Talk of the Town: Notes and Comment," The New Yorker, XIII (April 3, 1937), 11-12.

"The Talk of the Town: Notes and Comment," The New Yorker, XIII (April 10, 1937), 13-14.

"The Talk of the Town: Notes and Comment," The New Yorker, XIII (April 17, 1937), 13-14.

"Department of Correction, Amplification, and Abuse," The New Yorker, XIII (April 17, 1937), 59-62. (Signed "P. B. Publico.")

"The Talk of the Town: Notes and Comment," The New Yorker, XIII (April 24, 1937), 11-12.

"The Talk of the Town: Notes and Comment," The New Yorker, XIII (May 1, 1937), 13-14.

"The Talk of the Town: Notes and Comment," The New Yorker, XIII (May 8, 1937), 9-10.

"The Talk of the Town: Notes and Comment," The New Yorker, XIII (May 15, 1937), 15-16.

"The Talk of the Town: Notes and Comment," The New Yorker, XIII (May 22, 1937), 11-12.

"The Talk of the Town: Notes and Comment," The New Yorker, XIII (May 29, 1937), 11-12.

"The Old Open Busses," The New Yorker, XIII (May 29, 1937), 24.*

"The Talk of the Town: Notes and Comment," The New Yorker, XIII (June 5, 1937), 13-14.

"The Talk of the Town: Notes and Comment," The New Yorker, XIII (June 12, 1937), 11-12.

"My Physical Handicap, Ha Ha," The New Yorker, XIII (June 12, 1937), 20.*

"City Evening," Library Journal, LXII (June 15, 1937), 509.

"The Talk of the Town: Notes and Comment," The New Yorker, XIII (June 19, 1937), 9-10.

"The Talk of the Town: Notes and Comment," The New Yorker, XIII (June 26, 1937), 13-14.

"The Talk of the Town: Notes and Comment," The New Yorker, XIII (July 3, 1937), 7-8.

"The Talk of the Town: Notes and Comment," The New Yorker, XIII (July 10, 1937), 7-8.

"Preposterous Parables: I. The Man Who Changed in Appearance," The New Yorker, XIII (July 10, 1937), 17.*

"The Talk of the Town: Notes and Comment," The New Yorker, XIII (July 17, 1937), 9-10.

"Preposterous Parables: II. The Strike at the Leisure Plant," The New Yorker, XIII (July 17, 1937), 26.*

"The Talk of the Town: Notes and Comment," The New Yorker, XIII (July 24, 1937), 9-10.

"The Talk of the Town: Notes and Comment," The New Yorker, XIII (July 31, 1937), 7-8.

"Preposterous Parables: III. The Family Which Dwelt Apart," The New Yorker, XIII (July 31, 1937), 17-18.*

"The Talk of the Town: Notes and Comment," The New Yorker, XIII (August 7, 1937), 9-10.

"Small Thanks to You," The New Yorker, XIII (November 27, 1937), 21.*

1938

"Liberal in a Lounge Chair," The New Yorker, XIV (February 19, 1938), 19-20.*

"Onward and Upward with the Arts: Fifty-two American Moods," The New Yorker, XIV (March 26, 1938), 21-24.

"The Talk of the Town: Notes and Comment," The New Yorker, XIV (April 2, 1938), 9-10.

"How the Automobile Got into Bermuda," The New Yorker, XIV (April 9, 1938), 22-23.*

"The Birth of an Adult," The New Yorker, XIV (April 23, 1938), 20-21. (Unsigned.)

"R. F. Tweedle D.," The New Yorker, XIV (May 14, 1938), 18.*

"Green Hill Far Away," The New Yorker, XIV (July 2, 1938), 16-17.*

"Daniel Webster, The Hay Fever and Me," *The New Yorker*, SIV (July 30, 1938), 14-15.*

"The Talk of the Town: Notes and Comment," *The New Yorker*, XIV (September 3, 1938), 7-8.

"The Talk of the Town: Notes and Comment," *The New Yorker*, XIV (September 10, 1938), 13-14.

"One Man's Meat," *Harper's Magazine*, CLXXVII (October, 1938), 553-556.

"The Talk of the Town: Notes and Comment," *The New Yorker*, XIV (October 29, 1938), 13-14.

"For Your Information, Senator...," *The New Yorker*, XIV (November 5, 1938), 47.

"One Man's Meat," *Harper's Magazine*, CLXXVII (November, 1938), 665-668.

"One Man's Meat," *Harper's Magazine*, CLXXVIII (December, 1938), 105-108.

1939

"One Man's Meat," *Harper's Magazine*, CLXXVIII (January, 1939), 217-220.

"The Talk of the Town: Notes and Comment," *The New Yorker*, XIV (January 7, 1939), 9-10.

"The Talk of the Town: Notes and Comment," *The New Yorker*, XIV (January 28, 1939), 9-10.

"One Man's Meat: The Sixth Avenue El," *Harper's Magazine*, CLXXVIII (February, 1939), 329-332.

"Speaking of Counterweights," *The New Yorker*, XV (February 25, 1939), 19-22.*

"One Man's Meat: Farming Under Water, Etc.," *Harper's Magazine*, CLXXVIII (March, 1939), 441-444.

"The Talk of the Town: Notes and Comment," *The New Yorker*, XV (March 4, 1939), 11-12.

"The Talk of the Town: Notes and Comment," The New Yorker, XV (March 11, 1939), 15-16.

"The Door," The New Yorker, XV (March 25, 1939), 17-18.

"One Man's Meat: Sunday Morning Radio," Harper's Magazine, CLXXVIII (April, 1939), 553-556.

"The Talk of the Town: Notes and Comment," The New Yorker, XV (April 1, 1939), 11-12.

"The Talk of the Town: Notes and Comment," The New Yorker, XV (April 8, 1939), 11-12.

"The Talk of the Town: Notes and Comment," The New Yorker, XV (April 22, 1939), 11-12.

"One Man's Meat: Trees for Radio City," Harper's Magazine, CLXXVIII (May, 1939), 665-668.

"A Reporter at Large: They Come with Joyous Song," The New Yorker, XV (May 13, 1939), 25-28.

"Breakfast with Dorothy Thompson," The New Yorker, XV (May 27, 1939), 19-20.

"One Man's Meat," Harper's Magazine, CLXXIX (June, 1939), 105-108.

"The Talk of the Town: Notes and Comment," The New Yorker, XV (June 3, 1939), 11-12.

"The Talk of the Town: Notes and Comment," The New Yorker, XV (June 10, 1939), 11-12.

"One Man's Meat: Hollywood and a Nervous Dog," Harper's Magazine, CLXXIX (July, 1939), 217-220.

"The Talk of the Town: Notes and Comment," The New Yorker, XV (July 8, 1939), 15-16.

"Preposterous Parables: IV. Belford's Dash," The New Yorker, XV (July 22, 1939), 18.*

"The Talk of the Town: Notes and Comment," The New Yorker, XV (July 29, 1939), 9-10.

"One Man's Meat: Take a Letter to Thoreau," Harper's Magazine, CLXXIX (August, 1939), 329-332.

"The Talk of the Town: Notes and Comment," The New Yorker, XV (August 5, 1939), 7-8.

"The Talk of the Town: Notes and Comment," The New Yorker, XV (August 26, 1939), 9-10.

"One Man's Meat: With Asterisks," Harper's Magazine, CLXXIX (September, 1939), 441-444.

"The Talk of the Town: Notes and Comment," The New Yorker, XV (September 2, 1939), 11-12.

"The Talk of the Town: Notes and Comment," The New Yorker, XV (September 16, 1939), 17-18.

"The Talk of the Town: Notes and Comment," The New Yorker, XV (September 30, 1939), 11-12.

"One Man's Meat: Dr. Townsend Himself," Harper's Magazine, CLXXIX (October, 1939), 553-556.

"One Man's Meat: Lobstering and Freedom, Etc.," Harper's Magazine, CLXXIX (November, 1939), 665-668.

"The Flocks We Watch by Night," The New Yorker, XV (November 11, 1939), 20-21.*

"One Man's Meat: A War-Time Diary," Harper's Magazine, CLXXX (December, 1939), 105-108.

"Memoirs of a Master," The New Yorker, XV (December 23, 1939), 21-30. (Signed "M. R. A.")

1940

"One Man's Meat: Electric Fences, Poets, Etc.," Harper's Magazine, CLXXX (January, 1940), 217-220.

"One Man's Meat: Town Report--A Plan for America," Harper's Magazine, CLXXX (February, 1940), 329-332.

"The Talk of the Town: Notes and Comment," The New Yorker, XV (February 3, 1940), 13-14.

"One Man's Meat: Pale Hands, Form 1040, Search for a Sleigh, Etc.," Harper's Magazine, CLXXX (March, 1940), 441-444.

"The Talk of the Town: Notes and Comment," The New Yorker, XVI (March 2, 1940), 9-10.

"The Talk of the Town: Notes and Comment," The New Yorker, XVI (March 9, 1940), 13-14.

"Huntsman, I'm in a Quarry," Country Life, LXXVII (April, 1940), 45, 101.

"One Man's Meat," Harper's Magazine, CLXXX (April, 1940), 553-556.

"Our Contentious Readers," The New Yorker, XVI (April 6, 1940: 71-72. (Signed "Walter Tithridge, M.D.")

"One Man's Meat," Harper's Magazine, CLXXX (May, 1940), 665-668.

"The Talk of the Town: Notes and Comment," The New Yorker, XVI (May 4, 1940), 13-14.

"The Talk of the Town: Notes and Comment," The New Yorker, XVI (May 18, 1940), 11-12.

"A Boy I Knew," The Reader's Digest, XXXVI (June, 1940), 33-36.

"One Man's Meat," Harper's Magazine, CLXXXI (June, 1940), 105-108.

"The Talk of the Town: Notes and Comment," The New Yorker, XVI (June 22, 1940), 11-12.

"One Man's Meat," Harper's Magazine, CLXXI (July, 1940), 217-220.

"The Talk of the Town: Still Waters," The New Yorker, XVI (July 27, 1940), 11.

"One Man's Meat," Harper's Magazine, CLXXI (August, 1940), 329-332.

"One Man's Meat," Harper's Magazine, CLXXI (September, 1940), 441-444.

"The Talk of the Town: Notes and Comment," The New Yorker, XVI (September 7, 1940), 13-14.

"The Talk of the Town: Notes and Comment," The New Yorker, XVI (September 14, 1940), 13-14.

"One Man's Meat: The Practical Farmer," Harper's Magazine, CLXXXI (October, 1940), 553-556.

"The Sevenfold Pooh," The New Yorker, XVI (October 19, 1940), 25.*

"One Man's Meat," Harper's Magazine, CLXXXI (November, 1940), 665-668.

"Dinner with Henry Luce," The New Yorker, XVI (November 2, 1940), 23.*

"The Talk of the Town: Notes and Comment," The New Yorker, XVI (November 16, 1940), 11-12.

"The Talk of the Town: Notes and Comment," The New Yorker, XVI (November 30, 1940), 11-12.

"One Man's Meat," Harper's Magazine, CLXXXII (December, 1940), 105-108.

1941

"One Man's Meat: Lime, Dogs, Etc.," Harper's Magazine, CLXXXII (January, 1941), 217-220.

"One Man's Meat: Reading Mrs. Lindbergh," Harper's Magazine, CLXXXII (February, 1941), 329-332.

"One Man's Meat," Harper's Magazine, CLXXXII (March, 1941), 441-444.

"White House Callers," The New Yorker, XVII (March 15, 1941), 19.*

"One Man's Meat," Harper's Magazine, CLXXXII (April, 1941), 553-556.

"One Man's Meat: I Take a Poll," Harper's Magazine, CLXXXII (May, 1941), 665-668.

"One Man's Meat: Spring, Stove, etc.," Harper's Magazine, CLXXXIII (June, 1941), 105-108.

"One Man's Meat: What Hitler Has Done," Harper's Magazine, CLXXXIII (July, 1941), 217-220.

"The Talk of the Town: Notes and Comment," The New Yorker, XVII (July 19, 1941), 7-8.

"One Man's Meat: My Day," Harper's Magazine, CLXXXIII (August, 1941), 329-332.

"One Man's Meat: Mr. Volente," Harper's Magazine, CLXXXIII (September, 1941), 441-444.

"One Man's Meat: Once More to the Lake," Harper's Magazine, CLXXXIII (October, 1941), 553-556.

"The Preaching Humorist," The Saturday Review of Literature, XXIV (October 18, 1941), 16, 37. (Excerpt from "Introduction" to A Subtreasury of American Humor.)

"One Man's Meat: County Fairs, Doctors," Harper's Magazine, CLXXXIII (November, 1941), 665-668.

"One Man's Meat: Today I Should," Harper's Magazine, CLXXXIV (December, 1941), 105-108.

"The Talk of the Town: Notes and Comment," The New Yorker, XVII (December 27, 1941), 7-8.

1942

"One Man's Meat: Coon Hunt," Harper's Magazine, CLXXXIV (January, 1942), 217-220.

"The Talk of the Town: Notes and Comment," The New Yorker, XVII (January 3, 1942), 9-10.

"One Man's Meat: With War Declared," Harper's Magazine, CLXXXIV (February, 1942), 329-332.

"One Man's Meat: Second Call to Arms," Harper's Magazine, CLXXXIV (March, 1942), 441-444.

"The Talk of the Town: Notes and Comment," *The New Yorker*, XVIII (March 14, 1942), 13-14.

"The Talk of the Town: Notes and Comment," *The New Yorker*, XVIII (March 28, 1941), 13-14.

"One Man's Meat: Love Affair with America," *Harper's Magazine*, CLXXXIV (April, 1942), 553-556.

"The Retort Transcendental," *The New Yorker*, XVIII (April 4, 1942), 12.

"The Talk of the Town: Notes and Comment," *The New Yorker*, XVIII (April 18, 1942), 9-10.

"One Man's Meat: Birds and a Blackout," *Harper's Magazine*, CLXXXV (June, 1942), 105-108.

"The Talk of the Town: Notes and Comment," *The New Yorker*, XVIII (June 27, 1942), 9-10.

"One Man's Meat," *Harper's Magazine*, CLXXXV (July, 1942), 217-220.

"One Man's Meat: Aunt Poo," *Harper's Magazine*, CLXXXV (August, 1942), 329-332.

"The Talk of the Town: Notes and Comment," *The New Yorker*, XVIII (August 1, 1942), 9-10.

"The Talk of the Town: Notes and Comment," *The New Yorker*, XVIII (August 8, 1942), 7-8.

"The Talk of the Town: Notes and Comment," *The New Yorker*, XVIII (August 15, 1942), 9-10.

"The Talk of the Town: Notes and Comment," *The New Yorker*, XVIII (August 22, 1942), 7-8.

"The Talk of the Town: Notes and Comment," *The New Yorker*, XVIII (August 29, 1942), 9-10.

"One Man's Meat: Testing the Prophets," *Harper's Magazine*, CLXXXV (September, 1942), 441-444.

"The Talk of the Town: Notes and Comment," *The New Yorker*, XVIII (September 12, 1942), 9-10.

"The Talk of the Town: Notes and Comment," The New Yorker, XVIII (September 19, 1942), 9-10.

"The Talk of the Town: Notes and Comment," The New Yorker, XVIII (September 26, 1942), 11-12.

"One Man's Meat: Morningtime and Eveningtime," Harper's Magazine, CLXXXV (October, 1942), 553-556.

"The Talk of the Town: Notes and Comment," The New Yorker, XVIII (October 3, 1942), 7-8.

"The Talk of the Town: Notes and Comment," The New Yorker, XVIII (October 10, 1942), 9-10.

"The Talk of the Town: Notes and Comment," The New Yorker, XVIII (October 17, 1942), 13-14.

"The Talk of the Town: Notes and Comment," The New Yorker, XVIII (October 24, 1942), 11-12.

"The Talk of the Town: Notes and Comment," The New Yorker, XVIII (October 31, 1942), 11-12.

"One Man's Meat: I Expect a Cow," Harper's Magazine, CLXXXV (November, 1942), 615-618.

"The Talk of the Town: Notes and Comment," The New Yorker, XVIII (November 14, 1942), 11-12.

"The Talk of the Town: Notes and Comment," The New Yorker, XVIII (November 21, 1942), 11-12.

"The Talk of the Town: Notes and Comment," The New Yorker, XVIII (November 28, 1942), 11-12.

"One Man's Meat: Lamour Sells Bonds," Harper's Magazine, CLXXXVI (December, 1942), 62-65.

"The Talk of the Town: Notes and Comment," The New Yorker, XVIII (December 12, 1942), 15-16.

"The Talk of the Town: Notes and Comment," The New Yorker, XVIII (December 26, 1942), 9-10.

1943

"One Man's Meat: Diary for a Week," Harper's Magazine, CLXXXVI (January, 1943), 164-168.

"The Talk of the Town: Notes and Comment," The New Yorker, XVIII (January 9, 1943), 9-10.

"The Talk of the Town: Notes and Comment," The New Yorker, XVIII (January 16, 1943), 9-10.

"The Talk of the Town: Notes and Comment," The New Yorker, XVIII (January 30, 1943), 9-10.

"One Man's Meat: The Century of Controls," Harper's Magazine, CLXXXVI (February, 1943), 292-296.

"The Talk of the Town: Notes and Comment," The New Yorker, XVIII (February 13, 1943), 9-10.

"The Talk of the Town: Notes and Comment," The New Yorker, XIX (February 20, 1943), 7-8.

"The Talk of the Town: Notes and Comment," The New Yorker, XIX (February 27, 2943), 9-10.

"One Man's Meat: Cold Weather," Harper's Magazine, CLXXXVI (March, 1943), 392-395.

"The Talk of the Town: Notes and Comment," The New Yorker, XIX (March 13, 1943), 11-12.

"The Talk of the Town: Notes and Comment," The New Yorker, XIX (March 20, 1943), 11-12.

"I Accept with Widespread Pleasure...," The New Yorker, XIX (March 20, 1943), 16.*

"The Talk of the Town: Notes and Comment," The New Yorker, XIX (March 27, 1943), 11-12.

"One Man's Meat," Harper's Magazine, CLXXXVI (April, 1943), 498-501.

"The Talk of the Town: Notes and Comment," The New Yorker, XIX (April 10, 1943), 11-12.

"The Talk of the Town: Notes and Comment," The New Yorker, XIX (April 17, 1943), 13-14.

"The Talk of the Town: Notes and Comment," The New Yorker, XIX (April 24, 1943), 9-10.

"One Man's Meat: In Central Park," Harper's Magazine, CLXXXVI (May, 1943), 596-598.

"The Talk of the Town: Notes and Comment," The New Yorker, XIX (May 1, 1943), 11-12.

"The Talk of the Town: Notes and Comment," The New Yorker, XIX (May 8, 1943), 11-12.

"The Talk of the Town: Notes and Comment," The New Yorker, XIX (May 15, 1943), 11-12.

"The Talk of the Town: Notes and Comment," The New Yorker, XIX (May 29, 1943), 13-14.

"The Talk of the Town: Notes and Comment," The New Yorker, XIX (June 12, 1943), 11-12.

"The Talk of the Town: Notes and Comment," The New Yorker, XIX (June 19, 1943), 13-14.

"The Talk of the Town: Notes and Comment," The New Yorker, XIX (June 26, 1943), 11-12.

"The Talk of the Town: Notes and Comment," The New Yorker, XIX (July 3, 1943), 13-14.

"The Talk of the Town: Notes and Comment," The New Yorker, XIX (July 10, 1943), 13-14.

"The Talk of the Town: Notes and Comment," The New Yorker, XIX (July 17, 1943), 13-14.

"The Life Triumphant," The New Yorker, XIX (July 17, 1943), 18-20.

"The Talk of the Town: Notes and Comment," The New Yorker, XIX (July 24, 1943), 11-12.

"The Talk of the Town: Notes and Comment," The New Yorker, XIX (July 31, 1943), 13-14.

"The Talk of the Town: Notes and Comment," The New Yorker, XIX (August 7, 1943), 11-12.

"The Talk of the Town: Notes and Comment," The New Yorker, XIX (August 14, 1943), 13-14.

"The Talk of the Town: Notes and Comment," The New Yorker, XIX (August 21, 1943), 13-14.

"The Talk of the Town: Notes and Comment," The New Yorker, XIX (August 28, 1943), 13-14.

"The Talk of the Town: Notes and Comment," The New Yorker, XIX (September 4, 1943), 11-12.

"The Talk of the Town: Notes and Comment," The New Yorker, XIX (September 11, 1943), 17-18.

"The Talk of the Town: Notes and Comment," The New Yorker, XIX (September 18, 1943), 17-18.

"The Talk of the Town: Notes and Comment," The New Yorker, XIX (September 25, 1943), 13-14.

"The Talk of the Town: Notes and Comment," The New Yorker, XIX (October 2, 1943), 15-16.

"The Talk of the Town: Notes and Comment," The New Yorker, XIX (October 16, 1943), 17-18.

"The Talk of the Town: Notes and Comment," The New Yorker, XIX (October 23, 1943), 15-16.

"The Talk of the Town: Notes and Comment," The New Yorker, XIX (October 30, 1943), 15-16.

"The Talk of the Town: Notes and Comment," The New Yorker, XIX (November 20, 1943), 17-18.

"The Talk of the Town: Notes and Comment," The New Yorker, XIX (December 11, 1943), 25-26.

"The Talk of the Town: Notes and Comment," The New Yorker, XIX (December 18, 1943), 17-18.

"The Talk of the Town: Notes and Comment," The New Yorker, XIX (December 25, 1943), 11-12.

1944

"The Talk of the Town: Notes and Comment," The New Yorker, XIX (January 8, 1944), 13-14.

"The Talk of the Town: Notes and Comment," The New Yorker, XIX (January 15, 1944), 13-14.

"The Talk of the Town: Notes and Comment," The New Yorker, XIX (January 22, 1944), 13-14.

"A Weekend with the Angels," The New Yorker, XIX (January 22, 1944), 18-20.

"The Talk of the Town: Notes and Comment," The New Yorker, XIX (January 29, 1944), 13-14.

"The Talk of the Town: Notes and Comment," The New Yorker, XIX (February 5, 1944), 15-16.

"The Talk of the Town: Notes and Comment," The New Yorker, XX (February 19, 1944), 15-16.

"The Talk of the Town: Notes and Comment," The New Yorker, XX (February 26, 1944), 15-16.

"The Talk of the Town: Notes and Comment," The New Yorker, XX (March 4, 1944), 15-16.

"The Talk of the Town: Notes and Comment," The New Yorker, XX (March 11, 1944), 17-18.

"The Talk of the Town: Notes and Comment," The New Yorker, XX (March 18, 1944), 19-20.

"The Talk of the Town: Notes and Comment," The New Yorker, XX (March 25, 1944), 21-22.

"The Talk of the Town: Notes and Comment," The New Yorker, XX (April 1, 1944), 15-16.

"The Talk of the Town: Notes and Comment," The New Yorker, XX (April 8, 1944), 17-18.

"The Talk of the Town: Notes and Comment," The New Yorker, XX (April 15, 1944), 15-16.

"The Talk of the Town: Notes and Comment," The New Yorker, XX (April 22, 1944), 17-18.

"The Talk of the Town: Notes and Comment," The New Yorker, XX (April 29, 1944), 15-16.

"The Talk of the Town: Notes and Comment," The New Yorker, XX (May 6, 1944), 19-20.

"The Talk of the Town: Notes and Comment," The New Yorker, XX (May 13, 1944), 19-20.

"The Talk of the Town: Notes and Comment," The New Yorker, XX (May 27, 1944), 19-20.

"The Talk of the Town: Notes and Comment," The New Yorker, XX (June 3, 1944), 17-18.

"The Talk of the Town: Notes and Comment," The New Yorker, XX (June 10, 1944), 15-16.

"The Talk of the Town: Notes and Comment," The New Yorker, XX (July 1, 1944), 13-14.

"The Talk of the Town: Notes and Comment," The New Yorker, XX (July 8, 1944), 13-14.

"The Talk of the Town: Notes and Comment," The New Yorker, XX (July 22, 1944), 11-12.

"The Talk of the Town: Notes and Comment," The New Yorker, XX (July 29, 1944), 13-14.

"The Talk of the Town: Notes and Comment," The New Yorker, XX (August 5, 1944), 11-12.

"The Talk of the Town: Notes and Comment," The New Yorker, XX (August 12, 1944), 13-14.

"The Talk of the Town: Notes and Comment," The New Yorker, XX (August 26, 1944), 13-14.

"The Talk of the Town: Notes and Comment," The New Yorker, XX (September 2, 1944), 11-12.

"The Talk of the Town: Notes and Comment," The New Yorker, XX (September 9, 1944), 17-18.

"The Talk of the Town: Notes and Comment," The New Yorker, XX (September 16, 1944), 15-16.

"The Talk of the Town: Notes and Comment," The New Yorker, XX (September 23, 1944), 15-16.

"The Talk of the Town: Notes and Comment," The New Yorker, XX (September 30, 1944), 15-16.

"The Talk of the Town: Notes and Comment," The New Yorker, XX (October 7, 1944), 13-14.

"The Talk of the Town: Notes and Comment," The New Yorker, XX (October 14, 1944), 15-16.

"The Talk of the Town: Notes and Comment," The New Yorker, XX (October 21, 1944), 21-22.

"The Talk of the Town: Notes and Comment," The New Yorker, XX (October 28, 1944), 15-16.

"Breakfast on Quaker Hill," The New Yorker, XX (October 28, 1944), 27.

"The Talk of the Town: Notes and Comment," The New Yorker, XX (November 4, 1944), 15-16.

"The Talk of the Town: Notes and Comment," The New Yorker, XX (November 11, 1944), 19-20.

"The Talk of the Town: Notes and Comment," The New Yorker, XX (November 25, 1944), 17-18.

"The Talk of the Town: Notes and Comment," The New Yorker, XX (December 2, 1944), 23-24.

"The Talk of the Town: Notes and Comment," The New Yorker, XX (December 9, 1944), 23-24.

"The Talk of the Town: Notes and Comment," The New Yorker, XX (December 16, 1944), 15-16.

"The Talk of the Town: Notes and Comment," The New Yorker, XX (December 23, 1944), 13-14.

"The Talk of the Town: Notes and Comment," The New Yorker, XX (December 30, 1944), 11-12.

1945

"The State of the States," Transatlantic, January, 1945, pp. 28-31.

"The Talk of the Town: Notes and Comment," The New Yorker, XX (January 6, 1945), 15-16.

"The Talk of the Town: Notes and Comment," The New Yorker, XX (January 13, 1945), 13-14.

"The Talk of the Town: Notes and Comment," The New Yorker, XX (January 20, 1945), 11-12.

"The Talk of the Town: Notes and Comment," The New Yorker, XX (January 27, 1945), 15-16.

"The Talk of the Town: Notes and Comment," The New Yorker, XX (February 3, 1945), 15-16.

"The Talk of the Town: Notes and Comment," The New Yorker, XX (February 10, 1945), 15-16.

"About Myself," The New Yorker, XX (February 10, 1945), 20.

"The Talk of the Town: Notes and Comment," The New Yorker, XXI (February 17, 1945), 13-14.

"The Talk of the Town: Notes and Comment," The New Yorker, XXI (February 24, 1945), 17-18.

"The Talk of the Town: Notes and Comment," The New Yorker, XXI (March 3, 1945), 15-16.

"The Talk of the Town: Notes and Comment," The New Yorker, XXI (March 10, 1945), 17-18.

"The Talk of the Town: Notes and Comment," The New Yorker, XXI (March 17, 1945), 21-22.

"The Talk of the Town: Notes and Comment," The New Yorker, XXI (March 24, 1945), 23-24.

"The Talk of the Town: Notes and Comment," The New Yorker, XXI (March 31, 1945), 15-16.

"The Talk of the Town: Notes and Comment," The New Yorker, XXI (April 7, 1945), 15-16.

"The Talk of the Town: Notes and Comment," The New Yorker, XXI (April 14, 1945), 15-16.

"The Talk of the Town: Notes and Comment," The New Yorker, XXI (April 21, 1945), 17-18.

"The Talk of the Town: Notes and Comment," The New Yorker, XXI (April 28, 1945), 15-16.

"The Talk of the Town: Notes and Comment," The New Yorker, XXI (May 5, 1945), 15-16.

"A Reporter at Large: The Eve of St. Francis," The New Yorker, XXI (May 5, 1945), 44-47.

"The Talk of the Town: Notes and Comment," The New Yorker, XXI (May 12, 1945), 15-16.

"A Reporter at Large: Beautiful upon a Hill," The New Yorker, XX (May 12, 1945), 44-47.

"The Talk of the Town: Notes and Comment," The New Yorker, XXI (May 19, 1945), 19-20.

"The Talk of the Town: Notes and Comment," The New Yorker, XXI (May 26, 1945), 15-16.

"The Talk of the Town: Notes and Comment," The New Yorker, XXI (June 2, 1945), 11-12.

"The Talk of the Town: Notes and Comment," The New Yorker, XXI (June 9, 1945), 13-14.

"The Talk of the Town: Notes and Comment," The New Yorker, XXI (June 16, 1945), 15-16.

"The Talk of the Town: Notes and Comment," The New Yorker, XXI (June 23, 1945), 13-14.

"The Talk of the Town: Notes and Comment," The New Yorker, XXI (June 30, 1945), 11-12.

"The Talk of the Town: Notes and Comment," The New Yorker, XXI (July 7, 1945), 13-14.

"The Talk of the Town: Notes and Comment," The New Yorker, XXI (July 14, 1945), 15-16.

"The Talk of the Town: Notes and Comment," The New Yorker, XXI (July 21, 1945), 9-10.

"The Talk of the Town: Notes and Comment," The New Yorker, XXI (July 28, 1945), 13-14.

"The Talk of the Town: Notes and Comment," The New Yorker, XXI (August 4, 1945), 11-12.

"The Talk of the Town: Notes and Comment," The New Yorker, XXI (August 11, 1945), 15-16.

"The Talk of the Town: Notes and Comment," The New Yorker, XXI (August 18, 1945), 13-14.

"The Talk of the Town: Notes and Comment," The New Yorker, XXI (August 25, 1945), 13-14.

"The Talk of the Town: Notes and Comment," The New Yorker, XXI (September 1, 1945), 13-14.

"The Talk of the Town: Notes and Comment," The New Yorker, XXI (September 8, 1945), 15-16.

"The Talk of the Town: Notes and Comment," The New Yorker, XXI (September 15, 1945), 17-18.

"The Talk of the Town: Notes and Comment," The New Yorker, XXI (October 13, 1945), 19-20.

"The Talk of the Town: Notes and Comment," The New Yorker, XXI (October 27, 1945), 15-16.

"The Talk of the Town: Notes and Comment," The New Yorker, XXI (November 3, 1945), 19-20.

"The Talk of the Town: Notes and Comment," The New Yorker, XXI (November 10, 1945), 19-20.

"The Talk of the Town: Notes and Comment," The New Yorker, XXI (November 24, 1945), 23-24.

"The Talk of the Town: Notes and Comment," The New Yorker, XXI (December 8, 1945), 25-26.

"The Talk of the Town: Notes and Comment," The New Yorker, XXI (December 22, 1945), 13-14.

"The Talk of the Town: Notes and Comment," The New Yorker, XXI (December 29, 1945), 11-12.

1946

"The Talk of the Town: Notes and Comment," The New Yorker, XXI (January 12, 1946), 17-18.

"The Talk of the Town: Notes and Comment," The New Yorker, XXI (January 19, 1946), 13-14.

"The Talk of the Town: Notes and Comment," The New Yorker, XXI (January 26, 1946), 15-16.

"The Talk of the Town: Notes and Comment," The New Yorker, XXI (February 2, 1946), 13-14.

"The Talk of the Town: Notes and Comment," The New Yorker, XXII (February 16, 1946), 23-25.

"The Talk of the Town: Notes and Comment," The New Yorker, XXII (February 23, 1946), 21-22.

"The Talk of the Town: Notes and Comment," The New Yorker, XXII (March 2, 1946), 15-16.

"The Talk of the Town: Notes and Comment," The New Yorker, XXII (March 9, 1946), 17-18.

"The Talk of the Town: Notes and Comment," The New Yorker, XXII (March 23, 1946), 19-20.

"Our Impressionable Readers," The New Yorker, XXII (March 23, 1946), 43.

"The Talk of the Town: Notes and Comment," The New Yorker, XXII (April 6, 1946), 19-21.

"The Talk of the Town: Notes and Comment," The New Yorker, XXII (April 13, 1946), 23-24.

"The Talk of the Town: Notes and Comment," The New Yorker, XXII (April 20, 1946), 21-22.

"The Talk of the Town: Notes and Comment," The New Yorker, XXII (April 27, 1946), 15-17.

"The Talk of the Town: Notes and Comment," The New Yorker, XXII (May 4, 1946), 17-18.

"The Talk of the Town: Notes and Comment," The New Yorker, XXII (May 11, 1946), 19-20.

"The Talk of the Town: Notes and Comment," The New Yorker, XXII (May 18, 1946), 17-18.

"The Talk of the Town: Notes and Comment," The New Yorker, XXII (June 1, 1946), 17-19.

"The Talk of the Town: Notes and Comment," The New Yorker, XXII (June 29, 1946), 13-14.

"The Talk of the Town: Notes and Comment," The New Yorker, XXII (July 13, 1946), 15-16.

"The Talk of the Town: Notes and Comment," The New Yorker, XXII (July 20, 1946), 13-14.

"The Talk of the Town: Notes and Comment," The New Yorker, XXII (August 10, 1946), 11-12.

"The Talk of the Town: Notes and Comment," The New Yorker, XXII (August 17, 1946), 13-14.

"The Talk of the Town: Notes and Comment," The New Yorker, XXII (October 5, 1946), 23-24.

"The Talk of the Town: Notes and Comment," The New Yorker, XXII (November 2, 1946), 23-24.

"The Talk of the Town: Notes and Comment," The New Yorker, XXII (November 9, 1946), 23-25.

"The Talk of the Town: Notes and Comment," The New Yorker, XXII (November 16, 1946), 23-24.

"The Talk of the Town: Notes and Comment," The New Yorker, XXII (November 23, 1946), 23-24.

"The Talk of the Town: Notes and Comment," The New Yorker, XXII (November 30, 1946), 31-32.

"The Talk of the Town: Notes and Comment," The New Yorker, XXII (December 7, 1946), 33-34.

"The Talk of the Town: Notes and Comment," The New Yorker, XXII (December 14, 1946), 33-34.

"The Talk of the Town: Notes and Comment," The New Yorker, XXII (December 21, 1946), 17-18.

"The Talk of the Town: Notes and Comment," The New Yorker, XXII (December 28, 1946), 15-16.

1947

"The Talk of the Town: Notes and Comment," The New Yorker, XXII (January 18, 1947), 19-20.

"Turtle Bay Diary," The New Yorker, XXIII (February 22, 1947), 70, 72, 74, 76.

"The Talk of the Town: Notes and Comment," The New Yorker, XXIII (March 1, 1947), 21-22.

"Turtle Bay Diary," The New Yorker, XXIII (March 1, 1947), 76.

"The Talk of the Town: Notes and Comment," The New Yorker, XXIII (March 8, 1947), 25-27.

"The Talk of the Town: Notes and Comment," The New Yorker, XXIII (March 15, 1947), 23-24.

"Go Jump in the Sea Dept.," The New Yorker, XXIII (March 29, 1947), 93-95. (Unsigned.)

"The Second Tree from the Corner," The New Yorker, XXIII (May 31, 1947), 22-24.

"Well, in the last chapter...," The New Yorker, XXIII (August 30, 1947), 55. (Unsigned.)

"The Talk of the Town: Notes and Comment," The New Yorker, XXIII (October 18, 1947), 27-28.

"The Talk of the Town: Notes and Comment," The New Yorker, XXIII (October 25, 1947), 23-24.

"Preposterous Parables: The Decline of Sport," The New Yorker, XXIII (October 25, 1947), 28-29.

"The Talk of the Town: Notes and Comment," The New Yorker, XXIII (November 1, 1947), 19-20.

"The Talk of the Town: Notes and Comment," The New Yorker, XXIII (November 8, 1947), 23-24.

"The Talk of the Town: Notes and Comment," The New Yorker, XXIII (November 22, 1947), 27-28.

"Afternoon of an American Boy," The New Yorker, XXIII (November 29, 1947), 38-40.

"The Talk of the Town: Notes and Comment," The New Yorker, XXIII (December 6, 1947), 33-34.

"The Talk of the Town: Notes and Comment," The New Yorker, XXIII (December 13, 1947), 25-26.

"The Talk of the Town: Notes and Comment," The New Yorker, XXIII (December 27, 1947), 15-16.

1948

"Death of a Pig," Atlantic Monthly, CLXXXI (January, 1948), 30-33.

"The Talk of the Town: Notes and Comment," The New Yorker, XXIII (January 17, 1948), 17-18.

"The Talk of the Town: Notes and Comment," The New Yorker, XXIII (January 24, 1948), 17-18.

"The Talk of the Town: Notes and Comment," The New Yorker, XXIII (January 31, 1948), 15-16.

"The Talk of the Town: Notes and Comment," The New Yorker, XXIII (February 7, 1948), 19-20.

"The Talk of the Town: Notes and Comment," The New Yorker, XXIII (February 14, 1948), 17-18.

"The Talk of the Town: Notes and Comment," The New Yorker, XXIV (February 21, 1948), 19-20.

"The Talk of the Town: Notes and Comment," The New Yorker, XXIV (March 13, 1948), 23-24.

"The Talk of the Town: Notes and Comment," The New Yorker, XXIV (March 20, 1948), 23-24.

"The Talk of the Town: Notes and Comment," The New Yorker, XXIV (April 3, 1948), 21-22.

"The Talk of the Town: Notes and Comment," The New Yorker, XXIV (April 10, 1948), 21-22.

"The Talk of the Town: Notes and Comment," The New Yorker, XXIV (April 17, 1948), 19-20.

"The Talk of the Town: Notes and Comment," The New Yorker, XXIV (April 24, 1948), 21-22.

"The Talk of the Town: Notes and Comment," The New Yorker, XXIV (May 1, 1948), 19-20.

"The Talk of the Town: Notes and Comment," The New Yorker, XXIV (May 8, 1948), 21-22.

"The Talk of the Town: Notes and Comment," The New Yorker, XXIV (May 29, 1948), 15-16.

"The Talk of the Town: Notes and Comment," The New Yorker, XXIV (June 5, 1948), 21-22.

"The Talk of the Town: Notes and Comment," The New Yorker, XXIV (June 12, 1948), 17-18.

"The Talk of the Town: Notes and Comment," The New Yorker, XXIV (June 19, 1948), 17-18.

"The Talk of the Town: Looks Low, Is Low," The New Yorker, XXIV (June 19, 1948), 21.

"The Talk of the Town: Notes and Comment," The New Yorker, XXIV (June 26, 1948), 17-18.

"The Talk of the Town: Notes and Comment," The New Yorker, XXIV (July 3, 1948), 15-16.

"The Talk of the Town: Notes and Comment," The New Yorker, XXIV (July 10, 1948), 11-12.

"The Talk of the Town: Notes and Comment," The New Yorker, XXIV (July 17, 1948), 17-18.

"The Talk of the Town: Notes and Comment," The New Yorker, XXIV (July 31, 1948), 13.

"The Talk of the Town: Notes and Comment," The New Yorker, XXIV (August 7, 1948), 13-14.

"The Talk of the Town: Notes and Comment," The New Yorker, XXIV (August 14, 1948), 17.

"The Talk of the Town: Notes and Comment," The New Yorker, XXIV (August 21, 1948), 19.

"The Talk of the Town: Notes and Comment," The New Yorker, XXIV (August 28, 1948), 13.

"The Talk of the Town: Notes and Comment," The New Yorker, XXIV (September 4, 1948), 15.

"The Talk of the Town: Notes and Comment," The New Yorker, XXIV (September 11, 1948), 23.

"The Talk of the Town: Notes and Comment," The New Yorker, XXIV (September 25, 1948), 23.

"The Talk of the Town: Notes and Comment," The New Yorker, XXIV (October 9, 1948), 21.

"The Talk of the Town: Notes and Comment," The New Yorker, XXIV (October 16, 1948), 23.

"The Talk of the Town: Notes and Comment," The New Yorker, XXIV (October 23, 1948), 23-24.

"The Talk of the Town: Notes and Comment," The New Yorker, XXIV (October 30, 1948), 15.

"The Talk of the Town: Notes and Comment," The New Yorker, XXIV (November 6, 1948), 23.

"The Talk of the Town: Notes and Comment," The New Yorker, XXIV (November 13, 1948), 21.

"The Talk of the Town: Notes and Comment," The New Yorker, XXIV (November 20, 1948), 31.

"The Talk of the Town: Notes and Comment," The New Yorker, XXIV (November 27, 1948), 23.

"The Talk of the Town: Notes and Comment," The New Yorker, XXIV (December 4, 1948), 25.

"The Talk of the Town: Notes and Comment," The New Yorker, XXIV (December 11, 1948), 25.

"The Talk of the Town: Notes and Comment," The New Yorker, XXIV (December 18, 1948), 19.

"The Talk of the Town: Notes and Comment," The New Yorker, XXIV (December 25, 1948), 11.

1949

"The Talk of the Town: Notes and Comment," The New Yorker, XXIV (January 1, 1949), 11-12.

"The Talk of the Town: Notes and Comment," The New Yorker, XXIV (January 8, 1949), 19.

"The Talk of the Town: Notes and Comment," The New Yorker, XXIV (January 29, 1949), 15-16.

"The Talk of the Town: Notes and Comment," The New Yorker, XXV (February 19, 1949), 21.

"The Talk of the Town: Notes and Comment," The New Yorker, XXV (February 26, 1949), 19.

"The Talk of the Town: Notes and Comment," The New Yorker, XXV (March 19, 1949), 21.

"The Talk of the Town: Notes and Comment," The New Yorker, XXV (March 26, 1949), 17-18.

"Here Is New York," Holiday, V (April, 1949), 34-41.

"The Talk of the Town: Notes and Comment," The New Yorker, XXV (April 16, 1949), 19.

"The Talk of the Town: Notes and Comment," The New Yorker, XXV (April 23, 1949), 17.

"The Talk of the Town: Notes and Comment," The New Yorker, XXV (May 7, 1949), 23.

"The Talk of the Town: Notes and Comment," The New Yorker, XXV (June 25, 1949), 15.

"Noontime of an Advertising Man," The New Yorker, XXV (June 25, 1949), 25-26.

"The Talk of the Town: Notes and Comment," The New Yorker, XXV (August 6, 1949), 13.

"The Talk of the Town: Notes and Comment," The New Yorker, XXV (August 13, 1949), 17.

"The Talk of the Town: Notes and Comment," The New Yorker, XXV (August 20, 1949), 15.

"The Talk of the Town: Notes and Comment," The New Yorker, XXV (August 27, 1949), 17.

"The Talk of the Town: Notes and Comment," The New Yorker, XXV (September 3, 1949), 17.

"The Talk of the Town: Notes and Comment," The New Yorker, XXV (September 10, 1949), 19-20.

"The Talk of the Town: Notes and Comment," The New Yorker, XXV (September 17, 1949), 23.

"The Talk of the Town: Notes and Comment," The New Yorker, XXV (September 24, 1949), 23-24.

"The Talk of the Town: Notes and Comment," The New Yorker, XXV (October 8, 1949), 19.

"The Talk of the Town: Notes and Comment," The New Yorker, XXV (October 15, 1949), 23.

"The Talk of the Town: Notes and Comment," The New Yorker, XXV (October 22, 1949), 23-24.

"The Talk of the Town: Notes and Comment," The New Yorker, XXV (October 29, 1949), 19.

"The Talk of the Town: Notes and Comment," The New Yorker, XXV (November 5, 1949), 25.

"The Talk of the Town: Notes and Comment," The New Yorker, XXV (November 12, 1949), 25.

"The Talk of the Town: Notes and Comment," The New Yorker, XXV (November 19, 1949), 25-26.

"The Talk of the Town: Notes and Comment," The New Yorker, XXV (November 26, 1949), 23-24.

"The Talk of the Town: Notes and Comment," The New Yorker, XXV (December 3, 1949), 27.

"The Talk of the Town: Notes and Comment," The New Yorker, XXV (December 10, 1949), 29-30.

"The Talk of the Town: Notes and Comment," The New Yorker, XXV (December 17, 1949), 19-20.

"The Talk of the Town: Notes and Comment," The New Yorker, XXV (December 24, 1949), 13.

"The Talk of the Town: Notes and Comment," The New Yorker, XXV (December 31, 1949), 11.

1950

"The Talk of the Town: Notes and Comment," The New Yorker, XXV (January 14, 1950), 17.

"The Talk of the Town: Notes and Comment," The New Yorker, XXV (January 28, 1950), 17.

"The Talk of the Town: Notes and Comment," The New Yorker, XXV (February 11, 1950), 19.

"A Note," The New Yorker, XXV (February 11, 1950), 31.

"The Talk of the Town: Notes and Comment," The New Yorker, XXVI (February 25, 1950), 21.

"The Morning of the Day They Did It," The New Yorker, XXVI (February 25, 1950), 27-33.

"The Talk of the Town: Notes and Comment," The New Yorker, XXVI (March 25, 1950), 21.

"A Federalist at Three A.M.," The Blue Flag, XIV (April, 1950), 4-6. (Published by the Students of Dalton School.)

"The Talk of the Town: Notes and Comment," The New Yorker, XXVI (August 26, 1950), 17.

"The Talk of the Town: Notes and Comment," The New Yorker, XXVI (September 23, 1950), 23.

"The Talk of the Town: Notes and Comment," The New Yorker, XXVI (September 30, 1950), 17.

"Across the Street and into the Grill," The New Yorker, XXVI (October 14, 1950), 28.

"The Talk of the Town: Notes and Comment," The New Yorker, XXVI (October 21, 1950), 23.

"The Talk of the Town: Notes and Comment," The New Yorker, XXVI (November 4, 1950), 37-38.

"The Talk of the Town: Notes and Comment," The New Yorker, XXVI (November 18, 1950), 39.

"The Talk of the Town: Notes and Comment," The New Yorker, XXVI (December 2, 1950), 35.

"The Talk of the Town: Notes and Comment," The New Yorker, XXVI (December 9, 1950), 29.

"The Talk of the Town: Notes and Comment," The New Yorker, XXVI (December 16, 1950), 23-24.

"The Talk of the Town: Notes and Comment," The New Yorker, XXVI (December 30, 1950), 11-12.

1951

"The Talk of the Town: Notes and Comment," The New Yorker, XXVI (January 6, 1951), 23-24.

"The Talk of the Town: Notes and Comment," The New Yorker, XXVI (January 13, 1951), 17.

"The Talk of the Town: Notes and Comment," The New Yorker, XXVI (January 20, 1951), 17.

"The Talk of the Town: Notes and Comment," The New Yorker, XXVII (February 17, 1951), 21.

"The Talk of the Town: Notes and Comment," The New Yorker, XXVII (February 24, 1951), 19.

"The Talk of the Town: Notes and Comment," The New Yorker, XXVII (March 3, 1951), 21-22.

"The Talk of the Town: Notes and Comment," The New Yorker, XXVII (March 10, 1951), 23.

"The Talk of the Town: Notes and Comment," The New Yorker, XXVII (March 24, 1951), 19.

"The Talk of the Town: Notes and Comment," The New Yorker, XXVII (March 31, 1951), 17.

"The Talk of the Town: Notes and Comment," The New Yorker, XXVII (April 14, 1951), 23.

"Two Letters, Both Open," The New Yorker, XXVII (April 21, 1951), 26-27.

"The Talk of the Town: Notes and Comment," The New Yorker, XXVII (April 28, 1951), 19-20.

"The Talk of the Town: Notes and Comment," The New Yorker, XXVII (May 5, 1951), 23.

"The Talk of the Town: Notes and Comment," The New Yorker, XXVII (May 12, 1951), 23.

"The Talk of the Town: Notes and Comment," The New Yorker, XXVII (May 19, 1951), 27-28.

"The Talk of the Town: Notes and Comment," The New Yorker, XXVII (May 26, 1951), 17.

"The Talk of the Town: Notes and Comment," The New Yorker, XXVII (June 2, 1951), 19.

"The Talk of the Town: Notes and Comment," The New Yorker, XXVII (June 16, 1951), 21.

"The Talk of the Town: Notes and Comment," The New Yorker, XXVII (June 23, 1951), 19.

"The Talk of the Town: Notes and Comment," The New Yorker, XXVII (June 30, 1951), 15.

"The Talk of the Town: Notes and Comment," The New Yorker, XXVII (August 4, 1951), 15.

"The Talk of the Town: Notes and Comment," The New Yorker, XXVII (September 22, 1951), 23.

"The Talk of the Town: Notes and Comment," The New Yorker, XXVII (October 13, 1951), 29.

"The Talk of the Town: Notes and Comment," The New Yorker, XXVII (October 20, 1951), 23.

"The Talk of the Town: Notes and Comment," The New Yorker, XXVII (October 27, 1951), 23-24.

"The Talk of the Town: Notes and Comment," The New Yorker, XXVII (November 3, 1951), 25-26.

"The Talk of the Town: Notes and Comment," The New Yorker, XXVII (November 10, 1951), 29.

"The Talk of the Town: Notes and Comment," The New Yorker, XXVII (November 24, 1951), 27.

"The Talk of the Town: Notes and Comment," The New Yorker, XXVII (December 1, 1951), 39.

"The Talk of the Town: Notes and Comment," The New Yorker, XXVII (December 8, 1951), 31-32.

"The Talk of the Town: Notes and Comment," The New Yorker, XXVII (December 22, 1951), 15-16.

"The Hour of Letdown," The New Yorker, XXVII (December 22, 1951), 20-21.

"The Talk of the Town: Notes and Comment," The New Yorker, XXVII (December 29, 1951), 9.

1952

"The Talk of the Town: Notes and Comment," The New Yorker, XXVII (January 12, 1952), 15-16.

"The Talk of the Town: Notes and Comment," The New Yorker, XXVII (January 19, 1952), 17-18.

"The Talk of the Town: Notes and Comment," The New Yorker, XXVII (January 26, 1952), 15-16.

"The Talk of the Town: Notes and Comment," The New Yorker, XXVII (February 9, 1952), 23.

"The Talk of the Town: Notes and Comment," The New Yorker, XXVIII (February 16, 1952), 23.

"The Talk of the Town: Notes and Comment," The New Yorker, XXVIII (February 23, 1952), 23.

"The Talk of the Town: Notes and Comment," The New Yorker, XXVIII (March 1, 1952), 17.

"The Talk of the Town: Notes and Comment," The New Yorker, XXVIII (March 8, 1952), 23.

"The Talk of the Town: Notes and Comment," The New Yorker, XXVIII (March 15, 1952), 21-22.

"The Talk of the Town: Notes and Comment," The New Yorker, XXVIII (March 22, 1952), 23.

"The Talk of the Town: Notes and Comment," The New Yorker, XXVIII (March 29, 1952), 23.

"The Talk of the Town: Notes and Comment," The New Yorker, XXVIII (April 19, 1952), 23.

"The Talk of the Town: Notes and Comment," The New Yorker, XXVIII (May 10, 1952), 23.

"The Talk of the Town: Notes and Comment," The New Yorker, XXVIII (June 7, 1952), 17.

"The Talk of the Town: Notes and Comment," The New Yorker, XXVIII (June 14, 1952), 23.

"The Talk of the Town: Notes and Comment," The New Yorker, XXVIII (July 12, 1952), 17.

"The Talk of the Town: Notes and Comment," The New Yorker, XXVIII (September 6, 1952), 29.

"The Talk of the Town: Notes and Comment," The New Yorker, XXVIII (September 13, 1952), 31.

"The Talk of the Town: Notes and Comment," The New Yorker, XXVIII (September 20, 1952), 29.

"The Talk of the Town: Notes and Comment," The New Yorker, XXVIII (September 27, 1952), 19.

"The Talk of the Town: Notes and Comment," The New Yorker, XXVIII (October 4, 1952), 23.

"The Talk of the Town: Notes and Comment," The New Yorker, XXVIII (October 18, 1952), 29.

"The Talk of the Town: Notes and Comment," The New Yorker, XXVIII (October 25, 1952), 23.

"The Talk of the Town: Notes and Comment," The New Yorker, XXVIII (November 1, 1952), 21.

"The Talk of the Town: Notes and Comment," The New Yorker, XXVIII (November 8, 1952), 23.

"Trade Winds: Comment," Saturday Review, XXXV (November 15, 1952), 6.

"The Talk of the Town: Notes and Comment," The New Yorker, XXVIII (November 15, 1952), 31-32.

"The Talk of the Town: Notes and Comment," The New Yorker, XXVIII (November 22, 1952), 31.

"The Talk of the Town: Notes and Comment," The New Yorker, XXVIII (November 29, 1952), 31.

"The Talk of the Town: Notes and Comment," The New Yorker, XXVIII (December 13, 1952), 29-30.

"The Talk of the Town: Notes and Comment," The New Yorker, XXVIII (December 20, 1952), 23.

"The Talk of the Town: Notes and Comment," The New Yorker, XXVIII (December 27, 1952), 11.

1953

"The Talk of the Town: Notes and Comment," The New Yorker, XXVIII (January 3, 1953), 9.

"The Talk of the Town: Notes and Comment," The New Yorker, XXVIII (January 10, 1953), 17.

"The Talk of the Town: Notes and Comment," The New Yorker, XXVIII (January 17, 1953), 17-18.

"The Talk of the Town: Notes and Comment," The New Yorker, XXVIII (January 24, 1953), 19.

"The Talk of the Town: Notes and Comment," The New Yorker, XXVIII (January 31, 1953), 17-18.

"The Talk of the Town: Notes and Comment," The New Yorker, XXIX (February 21, 1953), 23-24.

"The Talk of the Town: Notes and Comment," The New Yorker, XXIX (February 28, 1953), 17.

"The Talk of the Town: Notes and Comment," The New Yorker, XXIX (March 7, 1953), 19-20.

"The Talk of the Town: Notes and Comment," The New Yorker, XXIX (March 14, 1953), 23.

"The Talk of the Town: Notes and Comment," The New Yorker, XXIX (March 21, 1953), 27.

"The Talk of the Town: Notes and Comment," The New Yorker, XXIX (March 28, 1953), 23-24.

"The Talk of the Town: Notes and Comment," The New Yorker, XXIX (April 4, 1953), 23-24.

"The Talk of the Town: Notes and Comment," The New Yorker, XXIX (April 18, 1953), 23-24.

"The Talk of the Town: Notes and Comment," The New Yorker, XXIX (April 25, 1953), 21.

"The Talk of the Town: Notes and Comment," The New Yorker, XXIX (May 2, 1953), 21.

"The Talk of the Town: Notes and Comment," The New Yorker, XXIX (May 9, 1953), 23.

"The Talk of the Town: Notes and Comment," The New Yorker, XXIX (May 16, 1953), 23.

"Visitors to the Pond," The New Yorker, XXIX (May 23, 1953), 28-31.

"The Talk of the Town: Notes and Comment," The New Yorker, XXIX (June 20, 1953), 17.

"The Talk of the Town: Notes and Comment," The New Yorker, XXIX (July 18, 1953), 15-16.

"The Talk of the Town: Notes and Comment," The New Yorker, XXIX (July 25, 1953), 17.

"The Talk of the Town: Seeing So Many Fezzes...," The New Yorker, XXIX (July 25, 1953), 21.

"The Talk of the Town: Notes and Comment," The New Yorker, XXIX (August 1, 1953), 11.

"The Talk of the Town: Notes and Comment," The New Yorker, XXIX (August 8, 1953), 13.

"The Talk of the Town: Notes and Comment," The New Yorker, XXIX (September 12, 1953), 25.

"The Talk of the Town: Notes and Comment," The New Yorker, XXIX (October 31, 1953), 23.

"The Talk of the Town: Notes and Comment," The New Yorker, XXIX (November 14, 1953), 31.

"The Talk of the Town: Notes and Comment," The New Yorker, XXIX (November 28, 1953), 35-36.

"The Talk of the Town: Notes and Comment," The New Yorker, XXIX (December 5, 1953), 41.

"The Talk of the Town: Notes and Comment," The New Yorker, XXIX (December 12, 1953), 33.

"The Talk of the Town: Notes and Comment," The New Yorker, XXIX (December 19, 1953), 19.

"The Talk of the Town: Notes and Comment," The New Yorker, XXIX (December 26, 1953), 13.

1954

"The Talk of the Town: Notes and Comment," The New Yorker, XXIX (January 2, 1954), 11.

"The Talk of the Town: Notes and Comment," The New Yorker, XXIX (January 9, 1954), 17.

"The Talk of the Town: Notes and Comment," The New Yorker, XXIX (January 16, 1954), 17.

"The Talk of the Town: Notes and Comment," The New Yorker, XXIX (January 30, 1954), 15-16.

"The Talk of the Town: Notes and Comment," The New Yorker, XXIX (February 6, 1954), 21.

"The Talk of the Town: Notes and Comment," The New Yorker, XXIX (February 13, 1954), 21.

"The Talk of the Town: Notes and Comment," The New Yorker, XXX (February 20, 1954), 23-24.

"The Talk of the Town: Notes and Comment," The New Yorker, XXX (February 27, 1954), 23.

"The Talk of the Town: Notes and Comment," The New Yorker, XXX (March 6, 1954), 19.

"The Talk of the Town: Notes and Comment," The New Yorker, XXX (March 13, 1954), 21.

"The Talk of the Town: Notes and Comment," The New Yorker, XXX (March 20, 1954), 25.

"The Talk of the Town: Notes and Comment," The New Yorker, XXX (April 24, 1954), 23-24.

"The Talk of the Town: Notes and Comment," The New Yorker, XXX (May 1, 1954), 23.

"The Talk of the Town: Notes and Comment," The New Yorker, XXX (May 8, 1954), 21.

"The Talk of the Town: Notes and Comment," The New Yorker, XXX (May 22, 1954), 23-24.

"The Talk of the Town: Notes and Comment," The New Yorker, XXX (June 12, 1954), 19-20.

"The Talk of the Town: Notes and Comment," The New Yorker, XXX (June 19, 1954), 17.

"The Talk of the Town: Notes and Comment," The New Yorker, XXX (July 3, 1954), 13.

"The Talk of the Town: Notes and Comment," The New Yorker, XXX (July 17, 1954), 17.

"Walden--1954," The Yale Review, XLIV (September, 1954), 13-22.

"The Talk of the Town: Notes and Comment," The New Yorker, XXX (September 11, 1954), 29.

"Our Windswept Correspondents: The Eye of Edna," The New Yorker, XXX (September 25, 1954), 39-40, 42, 44, 50, 52-55.

"The Talk of the Town: Notes and Comment," The New Yorker, XXX (October 2, 1954), 23.

"The Talk of the Town: Notes and Comment," The New Yorker, XXX (November 6, 1954), 29.

"The Talk of the Town: Notes and Comment," The New Yorker, XXX (November 20, 1954), 33.

"The Talk of the Town: Notes and Comment," The New Yorker, XXX (December 4, 1954), 37-38.

"The Talk of the Town: Notes and Comment," The New Yorker, XXX (December 11, 1954), 29.

"The Talk of the Town: Notes and Comment," The New Yorker, XXX (December 18, 1954), 25-26.

"The Talk of the Town: Notes and Comment," The New Yorker, XXX (December 25, 1954), 13.

"Yule Neurosis Sifted in Report," The New Yorker, XXX (December 25, 1954), 19.

1955

"The Talk of the Town: Notes and Comment," *The New Yorker*, XXX (January 1, 1955), 11-12.

"The Talk of the Town: Notes and Comment," *The New Yorker*, XXX (January 15, 1955), 19-20.

"The Talk of the Town: Notes and Comment," *The New Yorker*, XXX (January 22, 1955), 21.

"The Talk of the Town: Notes and Comment," *The New Yorker*, XXX (February 5, 1955), 21-22.

"The Talk of the Town: Notes and Comment," *The New Yorker*, XXXI (February 19, 1955), 23-24.

"The Talk of the Town: Notes and Comment," *The New Yorker*, XXXI (March 19, 1955), 29-30.

"The Talk of the Town: Notes and Comment," *The New Yorker*, XXXI (April 9, 1955), 23.

"The Talk of the Town: Notes and Comment," *The New Yorker*, XXXI (April 16, 1955), 29-30.

"The Talk of the Town: Notes and Comment," *The New Yorker*, XXXI (April 30, 1955), 23.

"The Talk of the Town: Notes and Comment," *The New Yorker*, XXXI (June 11, 1955), 23.

"The Talk of the Town: Notes and Comment," *The New Yorker*, XXXI (June 18, 1955), 17.

"The Talk of the Town: Notes and Comment," *The New Yorker*, XXXI (July 30, 1955), 17.

"The Talk of the Town: Notes and Comment," *The New Yorker*, XXXI (October 8, 1955), 35-36.

"An Old Coon Dog Scolds a Pup," *Life*, XXXIX (November 14, 1955), 192.

"Letter from the East," *The New Yorker*, XXXI (December 24, 1955), 60-64.*

1956

"Letter from the East," The New Yorker, XXXI (February 18, 1956), 72, 74, 76, 78, 80-85.*

"A Stratagem for Retirement," Holiday, XIX (March, 1956), 84-87.

"Letter from the South," The New Yorker, XXXII (April 7, 1956), 39-40, 42, 44, 47-49.

"Letter from the East," The New Yorker, XXXII (June 30, 1956), 33-34, 36, 39-41, 44-46.

"The Talk of the Town: Notes and Comment," The New Yorker, XXXII (September 22, 1956), 35.

"Letter from the East," The New Yorker, XXXII (November 3, 1956), 186-195.

"Letter from the East," The New Yorker, XXXII (December 15, 1956), 43-44, 46, 49-51.

"The Talk of the Town: Notes and Comment," The New Yorker, XXXII (December 22, 1956), 15.

1957

"The Talk of the Town: Notes and Comment," The New Yorker, XXXIII (February 16, 1957), 23-24.

"The Talk of the Town: Notes and Comment," The New Yorker, XXXIII (February 23, 1957), 23-25.

"The Talk of the Town: Notes and Comment," The New Yorker, XXXIII (March 2, 1957), 23-24.

"Answers to Hard Questions," The New Yorker, XXXIII (May 4, 1957), 29-30.

"Letter from the East," The New Yorker, XXXIII (May 25, 1957), 135-136.

"Letter from the East," The New Yorker, XXXIII (July 27, 1957), 35-36, 41-45.*

"The Seven Steps to Heaven," The New Yorker, XXXIII (September 7, 1957), 32-37.

"The Talk of the Town: Notes and Comment," The New Yorker, XXXIII (September 21, 1957), 33.

"The Talk of the Town: Notes and Comment," The New Yorker, XXXIII (October 26, 1957), 33.

"Fred on Space," The New Yorker, XXXIII (November 16, 1957), 46-47.

"Letter from the East," The New Yorker, XXXIII (November 23, 1957), 145-148.

1958

"Letter from the East," The New Yorker, XXXIV (February 22, 1958), 31-35.

"Letter from the North," The New Yorker, XXXIV (April 5, 1958), 34-38.

1959

"Khrushchev and I," The New Yorker, XXXV (September 26, 1959), 39-41.

1960

"Letter from the East," The New Yorker, XXXVI (February 20, 1960), 42-49.

"The Talk of the Town: Notes and Comment," The New Yorker, XXXVI (April 2, 1960), 31.

"Letter from the West," The New Yorker, XXXVI (June 18, 1960), 32-38.

"Letter from the East," The New Yorker, XXXVI (December 3, 1960), 233-248.

1961

"The Talk of the Town: Notes and Comment," The New Yorker, XXXVII (February 18, 1961), 30.

"Letter (Delayed) from the North," The New Yorker, XXVII (March 25, 1961), 47-110.

"Department of Amplification," The New Yorker, XXXVII (August 5, 1961), 42-45.

1963

"The Sea and the Wind That Blows," Ford Times, LVI (June, 1963), 2-6.

"The Talk of the Town: Notes and Comment," The New Yorker, XXXIX (October 26, 1963), 39.

"The Talk of the Town: Notes and Comment," The New Yorker, XXXIX (November 30, 1963), 49-51.

1964

"The Talk of the Town: Notes and Comment," The New Yorker, XL (May 2, 1964), 35.

"The Talk of the Town: Notes and Comment," The New Yorker, XL (May 9, 1964), 33.

"Was Lifted by Ears as Boy, No Harm Done," The New Yorker, XL (May 9, 1964), 38.

"The Talk of the Town: Notes and Comment," The New Yorker, XL (October 3, 1964), 43.

"The Talk of the Town: Notes and Comment," The New Yorker, XL (October 24, 1964), 47.

"The Talk of the Town: Notes and Comment," The New Yorker, XL (December 12, 1964), 45.

1965

"The Talk of the Town: Notes and Comment," The New Yorker, XL (January 23, 1965), 25.

"The Talk of the Town: Notes and Comment," The New Yorker, XLI (March 20, 1965), 35.

"The Talk of the Town: Notes and Comment," The New Yorker, XLI (March 27, 1965), 35.

1966

"What Do Our Hearts Treasure?" The New Yorker, XLI (January 15, 1966), 29-30.

"Annals of Birdwatching: Mr. Forbush's Friends," The New Yorker, XLII (February 26, 1966), 42-66.

"The Librarian Said It Was Bad for Children," The New York Times, March 6, 1966, II, p. 19.

"The Talk of the Town: Notes and Comment," The New Yorker, XLII (October 1, 1966), 41-42.

1967

"Topics: Dear Mr. [illegible] The New York Times, September 23, 1967, p. 30.

"Topics: An Act of Intellect to Turn the Year," The New York Times, December 30, 1967, p. 22.

1968

"Topics: Our New Countryman at the U.N.," The New York Times, October 12, 1968, p. 36.

1969

"[An Account of How He Spent the Day, October 12, 1968]" Haggis/Bagis, (Winter, 1969), pp. [27]-[28] (Miss Porter's School, Framington, Conn.)

"The Talk of the Town: Notes and Comment," The New Yorker, XLV (April 12, 1969), 37.

"The Talk of the Town: Notes and Comment," The New Yorker, XLV (July 26, 1969), 25.

"The Talk of the Town: Notes and Comment," The New Yorker, XLV (October 11, 1969), 43.

1970

"In Charlie's Bar," The New Yorker, XLVI (February 21, 1970), 36.

"Laura Ingalls Wilder Acceptance, Address, June 30, 1970," Horn Book, XLVI (August, 1970), 349-351.

"I Paint What I See," Ramparts Magazine, IX (September, 1970), 34.

"The Browning-Off of Pelham Manor," The New Yorker, XLVI (November 14, 1970), 49.

1971

"Letter from the East," The New Yorker, XLVII (March 27, 1971), 35-37.

"The Talk of the Town: Notes and Comment," The New Yorker, XLVII (June 19, 1971), 19.

"Letter from the East," The New Yorker, XLVII (July 24, 1971), 27-29.

"Faith of a Writer: Remarks Upon Receiving the 1971 National Medal for Literature," Publishers Weekly, December 6, 1971, p. 29.

"The Egg Is All," The New York Times, December 7, 1971, p. 19.

1972

"The Talk of the Town: Notes and Comment," The New Yorker, XLVIII (December 2, 1972), 45.

1973

"Goings On in the Barnyard," The New York Times, August 15, 1973, p. 37.

1974

"Downhill All the Way," The New York Times, January 16, 1974, p. 39.

"The Talk of the Town: Notes and Comment," The New Yorker, L (July 15, 1974), 23.

"The Talk of the Town: Notes and Comment," The New Yorker, L (July 29, 1974), 25.

1975

"Letter from the East," The New Yorker, LI (February 24, 1975), 36-40.

1976

"White's Letter to Ellsworth American," Authors Guild Bulletin, March-May, 1976, p. 6. Also appears under the title "Buy a Reporter" in The Boston Globe, January 1, 1976, p. 23.

"White's Letter to Xerox," Authors Guild Bulletin, March-May, 1976, pp. 7-8. Also appears in The Boston Globe, July 5, 1976, p. 33.

EDITORIALS

1917

"Editorial," High School Oracle (Mount Vernon, N.Y.), XVII (January-February, 1917), 15-16.

"Editorial," High School Oracle (Mount Vernon, N.Y.), XVII (May-June, 1917), 4-5.

1920

The following editorials appear in the Cornell Daily Sun on page 4, unless otherwise noted.

January 12, 1920: "Editorial: The Vile Vendetta of the...."

February 16, 1920: "Jacob Gould Sherman, Cornellian."

February 23, 1920: "Those Locker Coupons."

March 8, 1920: "To Bust or Not to Bust."

March 10, 1920: "A School of Journalism at Cornell."

March 15, 1920: "Editorial: Whatever May Be the...."

March 22, 1920: "What Goes On."

March 29, 1920: "An Open Discussion."

April 6, 1920: "The Sun, 1920-1921," "The First Cornell President," p. 6.

April 7, 1920: "The Return of the Teams," "Dobie Arrives."

April 8, 1920: "A Stone Unturned," "Another Recruit," "The Anonymous Letter."

April 9, 1920: "A Revived Art," "Honor to Scholarship."

April 10, 1920: "Bon Voyage," "Biting the Hand That Feeds," "The Ubiquitous Canine."

April 12, 1920: "The Bashful Majority," "The Mutilated Cap."

April 13, 1920: "1921's Chance," "Lacrosse as a Game."

April 14, 1920: "New Rushing Rules."

April 15, 1920: "The Next Step," "A Hoover Meeting."

April 16, 1920: "Cornell Loses to Harvard," "Another Beaux Arts," "The World Is Heard From."

April 17, 1920: "The Festival Chorus," "Overall for Girls and Men," "Take a Vote."

April 19, 1920: "Why You Should Go," "Ice Water," "The Old Yell."

April 20, 1920: "When to Eat," "The Other 4,999."

April 21, 1920: "A Fad or a Fixture?"

April 22, 1920: "The Drill Schedule," "The Rising Mercury."

April 23, 1920: "A Senior Banquet," "The Serpent in the Gorge."

April 24, 1920: "Percy Field Today," "A Battle Royal," "The Critic."

April 26, 1920: "Prospectus," "A Student Judiciary."

April 27, 1920: "Have a Thought," "An Advanced Course."

April 28, 1920: "Journalism at Cornell," "The Athletic Tax."

April 29, 1920: "Breaking Training," "A Free Concert."

April 30, 1920: "The Straw Vote," "British Guests."

May 1, 1920: "Thomas Mott Osborne," "A Penn Game."

May 3, 1920: "Petition for Journalism," "What Is a Class?"

May 4, 1920: "Guests at Cornell," "Why a Bonus?" "The Funny Stands."

May 5, 1920: "Spring Football," "Rusty Pilots."

May 6, 1920: "The Council's Action," "Untrodden Ways."

May 7, 1920: "Why Minor Sport?"

May 8, 1920: "First of All, Good Citizenship."

May 10, 1920: "Honorary Society Eligibility," "Second Term Initiation."

May 11, 1920: "A Crew Send-Off," "Cornell Fabyan," "The Military Department."

May 12, 1920: "Public Speaking," "The Fall Creek Natatorium."

May 13, 1920: "Start Running," "Beer and the Constitution."

May 14, 1920: "The Music Festival," "How Big Is Cornell?" "The Crew Send-Off."

May 15, 1920: "Figure It Out," "Freshman Tax."

May 17, 1920: "Cornell Crew Got Stuck in the Grass," "Sunday Baseball."

May 18, 1920: "The King's English," "The Observation Train."

May 19, 1920: "Supervising the College Man," "Bolstering Up Tradition," "Percy Field Will Be Ready."

May 20, 1920: "Council Elections," "A Ball Playing Crowd."

May 21, 1920: "Syracuse--Cornell," "The Fate of a System."

May 22, 1920: "The Old Boys Cavort," "How Many Students," "Cornell Rows Harvard."

May 24, 1920: "The Lacrosse Season," "Exchange Classes," "What Is Cheerleading?"

May 25, 1920: "David Starr Jordan," "What to Wear."

May 26, 1920: "Poughkeepsie at Poughkeepsie."

May 27, 1920: "Lack of Discipline."

May 28, 1920: "Another Failure," "Production."

May 29, 1920: "Percentage of Women," "Back to the Farm."

May 31, 1920: "The X in Examination."

June 1, 1920: "The Professor's Job," "Nick Bawlf."

September 27, 1920: "Point of View," "Charles E. Courtney."

September 28, 1920: "Rushing," "A Quarter of a Million."

September 29, 1920: "Probation," "A Sporting Chance."

September 30, 1920: "The Semi-Annual Mercy," "The Competitive System."

October 1, 1920: "Freshman Rules," "On Listening Ears," "Little Lessons in Probation."

October 2, 1920: "A President for Cornell," "Little Lessons in Probation."

October 4, 1920: "A Sporting Proposition," "Little Lessons in Probation."

October 5, 1920: "A Matter of Opinion," "Little Lessons in Probation," "Who Buys?"

October 6, 1920: "The Association Plans," "Little Lessons in Probation."

October 7, 1920: "They Shall Not Pass," "Little Lessons in Probation," "Absentee Voters."

October 8, 1920: "Good Votes Lost," "Little Lessons in Probation," "Line Forms in Front of Morrill."

October 9, 1920: "The Makings of a Union."

October 11, 1920: "Schuman and the League," "The Traction Corporation."

October 12, 1920: "The Cornell Spirit," "Non-Negotiable."

October 13, 1920: "A Fair Judgment," "Disquieting Figures."

October 14, 1920: "Two Kinds of Athletics," "Morrill Hospitality."

October 15, 1920: "Governor Alfred E. Smith," "The Right Balance."

October 16, 1920: "Eligibility," "The Law of the Land."

October 18, 1920: "Where Is Tennis?" "Sixty to Nothing."

October 19, 1920: "Council Elections," "The Passing of the Wet One."

October 20, 1920: "A Pledge in Good Faith," "The Respectability of the Drag," "An Intercollegiate Vote."

October 21, 1920: "Charles Love Durham '99," "The Miracle of the Classroom."

October 22, 1920: "Hollis E. Dann," "The Anomaly of the Co-Ed," "A Tennis Association."

October 23, 1920: "The Spoken Word," "Hello."

October 25, 1920: "The Phenomenon of the Cork Smeller," "The Rush," "Another Unit."

October 26, 1920: "The Square Thing," "Football."

October 27, 1920: "John Hoyle," "And Great Was the Noise Thereof."

October 28, 1920: "Saturday Night."

October 30, 1920: "An Embryo Classic," "A Noise for Dartmouth," "Basketball Competition."

November 1, 1920: "Cornell Victorious," "A Cheering Section," "The Hallowe'en Rush."

November 2, 1920: "Daniel Roars with Laughter."

November 3, 1920: "The Election," "When the Team Goes," "A Back Debt."

November 4, 1920: "Headlines," "Undeserved Bricks."

November 5, 1920: "Lots of Candidates," "New York Alumni."

November 6, 1920: "A Man without a Title," "The Baily Hall Game."

November 8, 1920: "A Fair Defeat," "The Tragedy of the Unimpassioned."

November 9, 1920: "A Cheering Section," "For Mutual Benefit."

November 10, 1920: "A Football Captain," "Spare Rooms."

November 11, 1920: "Armistice Day," "The Poor Pole."

November 12, 1920: "The Cheerful Yawner," "A Little Harmony," "Foibles of 1840."

November 13, 1920: "Visiting Teams," "The Scrub," "Cornell Daylight Saving."

November 15, 1920: "Too Soon Forgotten," "Food for Thought."

November 16, 1920: "Commercialized Football."

November 17, 1920: "Northwestern," "Leacock's University," "They're Off!"

November 18, 1920: "Artificial Rinks," "Harvard's System."

November 19, 1920: "The Faculty Tea Party," "Cornell-Dartmouth."

November 20, 1920: "The Little Penn Game," "Past and Present."

November 22, 1920: "Cross Country," "Cornell Hospitality."

November 23, 1920: "A Courtney Memorial," "Joint Meetings."

November 24, 1920: "Dexter S. Kimball," "Beds for Boys," "The Lure of the Sea."

November 26, 1920: "Football and Psychology."

November 27, 1920: "Next Year's Rushing."

November 29, 1970: "The Tempestuous Teapot."

November 30, 1920: "The Cornell Era," "A Ratio of Colleges."

December 1, 1920: "The Higher the Drier," "Blue Laws."

December 2, 1920: "John J. Carney," "The Muddy Stream," "Repudiation."

December 3, 1920: "And Jake Begat John...," "Superficiality."

December 4, 1920: "Non-Fraternity."

December 6, 1920: "Five Little Lessons," "Independent Organization," "Winter Sports."

December 7, 1920: "The Cornell Era," "For They Teach Not Their Own Use."

December 8, 1920: "A Step toward a Goal," "Cross Country Championship."

December 9, 1920: "The Leaderless Team," "To Do It Well and Not for Gain."

December 10, 1920: "Training for Officers," "Free Speech and Bad Judgment," "The Hungry Scufflers."

December 11, 1920: "Two Identical Parties."

December 13, 1920: "Let the Council Know," "Traction Service."

December 14, 1920: "Off for England," "Ourselves and Others."

December 15, 1920: "Page Mr. Moakley," "Walter Hampden," "Professor Stagg's Appointment."

December 16, 1920: "Senator Cartwright," "The Prelim Period," "Tell 'em the Truth."

December 17, 1920: "Sound Doctrine," "A Trial Blue Sunday."

December 18, 1920: "The Psychology of the Bull Session, or, The Professor in the Home."

December 20, 1920: "Three Hundred Years Ago," "Basketball Again."

December 21, 1920: "The Cotillion Game," "A Christmas Gift," "The Dear Old Stuff."

December 22, 1920: "A Pretty Good Place," "Barnes Hall Hospitality."

1921

January 6, 1921: "A Triumphant Defeat."

January 7, 1921: "What Will the Faculty Do?" "Hearths."

January 8, 1921: "The Crib Again."

January 10, 1921: "No Half Way Mark," "A Distinguished College."

January 11, 1921: "Ezra Cornell," "Welcome Home."

January 12, 1921: "Is This the Time?" "The Belligerent Balloonists."

January 13, 1921: "The Joke in the Constitution."

January 14, 1921: "And the Answer Is."

January 15, 1921: "Alumni Organization," "Hockey Again."

January 17, 1921: "Cornell's Share," "Cornell on Beebe."

January 18, 1921: "The Chivalry of Democracy," "Two Conclusions," "A Chance to Forget Prejudice."

January 19, 1921: "Two Meals Today," "The General Examination."

January 20, 1921: "The Soviet Teacher," "What of the Age?"

January 21, 1921: "The Red Blooded Reformers."

January 22, 1921: "Wanted--A Junior Week System."

February 10, 1921: "Cornell's Guests," "The Faculty Wants to Know," "Fire!"

February 11, 1921: "The Promenade," "Business and Education."

February 12, 1921: "A New Party," "Not Big But Great," "Meet Penn with Penn Tactics."

February 14, 1921: "The Hardy Band," "The Independent Tea Dance," "Excellence of Speech."

February 15, 1921: "Dobie Signs Again."

February 16, 1921: "The Vote on the Honor System."

February 17, 1921: "Farmer's Week," "Keep the Title," "The Last Minute Jam."

February 19, 1921: "The C. E. Cases," "The Decent Dance."

February 21, 1921: "The Newer Art," "How Far to Go."

February 22, 1921: "The Ethics Club."

February 23, 1921: "Daylight Saving."

February 24, 1921: "The Constitution," "A Job for the Council."

February 25, 1921: "What the Constitution Provides."

February 26, 1921: "Figures," "Passing Bad Paper."

February 28, 1921: "We Will Not Report."

March 1, 1921: "Education Revolutionized?"

March 3, 1921: "The Size of the Vote."

March 5, 1921: "The Constitution Passes."

March 7, 1921: "The Faculty Should Ratify," "Our Major Minor Sport."

March 8, 1921: "The Parolers."

March 9, 1921: "What Is at Stake?" "The Extra Hour."

March 10, 1921: "Make Good the Trust," p. 2.

March 11, 1921: "Hoover on the Job."

March 12, 1921: "Seniors Doing Lessons."

March 14, 1921: "Activity," "The Debate Team."

March 15, 1921: "It's Coming On."

March 17, 1921: "Social Life at Williams."

March 19, 1921: "The Musical Clubs."

March 21, 1921: "The Problem of Rushing."

March 22, 1921: "The Band Concert."

March 23, 1921: "Something for Seniors."

March 24, 1921: "Simpler Rushing," "Who Shall Decide?"

March 26, 1921: "The 'More Liberal' Plan."

March 28, 1921: "Mr. MacKenzie."

March 29, 1921: "The Basis of Rushing," "Inviting Disaster."

March 31, 1921: "Our Postponed Easter," "Colleges and Poets."

April 2, 1921: "Another Vicious Circle."

April 4, 1921: "Decide before Vacation," "The Syracuse Tragedy."

REVIEWS

THEATRE

1927

The New Yorker, I (June 25, 1927), 66-68. Reviews of The Woman in Bronze and Lombardi, Ltd. by Murray Philips, Talk About Girls by Andrew Tombes, Baby Mine, and Julius Caesar. (Signed "Saul Wright.")

The New Yorker, III (July 9, 1927), 40-41. Reviews of A Midsummer Night's Dream, Bare Facts of 1927, and Bottomland by Clarence Williams. (Signed "Saul Wright.")

The New Yorker, III (July 23, 1927), 34-37. Reviews of Padlocks of 1927 by Paul Gerard Smith et al., Rang Tang by Kaj Gynt, Africana by Donald Heyward, and Madam X by Alexandre Bisson and John Raphael.

The New Yorker, III (August 6, 1927), 32-34. Reviews of Abie's Irish Rose by Anne Nichols, Kiss Me by Derick Wulff and Max Simon, The Manhatters by Aline Erlanger and George S. Oppenheimer, and The Mating Season by William A. Grew.

1928

The New Yorker, IV (August 18, 1928), 36-38. Reviews of Earl Carroll's Vanities by Earl Carroll et al., Elmer Gantry by Patrick Kearney, and Guns by James Hagan.

The New Yorker, IV (August 25, 1928), 32. Reviews of The Song Writer by Crane Wilbur, The Front Page by Ben Hecht and Charles MacArthur, and He Understood Women by Frances Lynch and Michael Kallesser.

The New Yorker, IV (September 1, 1928), 36, 41. Reviews of Gang War by Willard Mack, The Big Pond by George Middleton and A. E. Thomas, Goin' Home by Ransom Rideout, Relations by Willard Mack.

The New Yorker, IV (September 8, 1928), 25-26. Reviews of Gentlemen of the Press by Ward Morehouse, The Money Lender by Roy Horniman, Ringside by Edward E. Paramore, Jr., Hyatt Daab, and George Abbott, Eva the Fifth, and Caravan by Clifford Pember and Ralph Culliman.

1931

The New Yorker, VII (August 1, 1931), 28-29. Review of Shoot the Works by Heywood Broun and Milton Raison. (Signed "S. Finny.")

The New Yorker, VII (December 5, 1931), 29-34. Reviews of The Good Fairy by Ferenc Molnar, In Times Square by Dobson L. Mitchell and Clyde North, Miss Gulliver Travels by George Ford and Ethel Taylor, After All by John Van Druten, The Firefly by Otto Harbach and Rudolph Friml, and Bloody Laughter by Ernest Toller.

The New Yorker, VII (December 19, 1931), 28-32. Reviews of 1931-- by Clair Sifton and Paul Sifton, The Passing Present by Gretchen Damrosch, Springtime for Henry by Benn W. Levy, The Second Comin' by George Bryant, and Little Women by Marian de Forest.

The New Yorker, VII (December 26, 1931), 24-26. Reviews of [Variety Show] and The Barretts of Wimpole Street by Rudolf Besier.

1932

The New Yorker, VII (January 2, 1932), 26-28. Reviews of Of Thee I Sing by George S. Kaufman, Morrie Ryskin, George Gershwin and Ira Gershwin, and Cold in Sables by Doris Anderson and Joseph Jackson.

The New Yorker, VIII (September 17, 1932), 26-30. Reviews of Here Today by George S. Oppenheimer, The Man Who Reclaimed His Head by Arthur Hammerstein and

L. Lawrence Weber, Best Years by Raymond Van Sickle, and Ballyhoo of 1932 by Norman B. Anthony.

The New Yorker, VIII (September 24, 1932), 26-28. Reviews of Flying Colors by Howard Dietz and Arthur Schwartz, and Clear All Wires by Samuel Spewack and Bella Spewack.

The New Yorker, VIII (October 1, 1932), 28. Reviews of The Stork Is Dead by Frederic Hatton and Fanny Hatton, Lilly Turner by Philip Dunning and George Abbott, and Triplets by Mark Linder.

The New Yorker, VIII (October 8, 1932), 26. Reviews of Success Story by John Howard Lawson, and Earl Carroll's Vanities by John McGowen, et al.

The New Yorker, VIII (October 15, 1932), 28. Reviews of When Ladies Meet by Rachel Crothers, Nona by Gladys Unger, and Ol' Man Satan by Donald Heywood.

1933

The New Yorker, IX (June 10, 1933), 24-26. Reviews of Uncle Tom's Cabin by G. L. Aiken and A. E. Thomas, and Tattle Tales by Frank Fay and Nick Copeland.

The New Yorker, IX (June 24, 1933), 24-26. Reviews of Shooting Star by Noel Pierce and Bernard C. Schoenfeld, and The Climax by Edward Locke.

The New Yorker, IX (July 22, 1933), 24. Reviews of John Ferguson by St. John Ervine, and Shady Lady by Estelle Morando.

CINEMA

1933

The New Yorker, IX (September 30, 1933), 46-47. Reviews of Thunder Over Mexico and other films.

The New Yorker, IX (October 7, 1933), 57-58. Reviews of Footlight Parade, Ann Vickers, Waltz Time, and Brief Moment.

BOOKS

1928

The New Yorker, IV (June 9, 1928), 88-89. Review of Sunset Gun by Dorothy Parker.

1930

The New Yorker, VI (October 25, 1930), 26. Review of Seed; A Novel of Birth Control by Charles G. Norris.

The New Yorker, VI (December 13, 1930), 26. Review of Individualism, Old and New by John Dewey.

1931

The New Yorker, VII (May 23, 1931), 14. Review of Fatal Interview; A Volume of Love Sonnets by Edna St. Vincent Millay.

1933

The New Yorker, IX (December 16, 1933), 27. Review of More Power to You! A Working Technique for Making the Most of Human Energy by Walter B. Pitkin.

1946

The New Yorker, XXII (March 16, 1946), 97-99. Review of The First Freedom by Morris L. Ernst.

The New Yorker, XXII (December 28, 1946), 64-65. Review of Walden by Henry David Thoreau.

1947

The New Yorker, XXIII (November 8, 1947), 124, 126-127, 130-131. Review of Peace or Anarchy by Cord Meyer, Jr.

1948

The New Yorker, XXIV (May 8, 1948), 104. Review of Malabar Farm by Louis Bromfield.

The New Yorker, XXIV (December 4, 1948), 171-177. Review of No Place to Hide by David Bradley.

1950

The New Yorker, XXVI (November 18, 1950), 178-180. Review of A Plan for Peace by Grenville Clark.

The New Yorker, XXVI (November 18, 1950: 180-185. Review of Our Foreign Policy by the U.S. Department of State.

1954

The New Yorker, XXX (February 20, 1954), 109-114. Review of But We Were Born Free by Elmer Davis.

FOREWORDS, INTRODUCTIONS, AND CONTRIBUTIONS TO THE WORKS OF OTHERS

"Introduction" to The Owl in the Attic by James Thurber. New York: Harper & Brothers, 1931.

"I'd Send My Son to Cornell," in Our Cornell, compiled by Raymond Floyd Howes. Ithaca, N.Y.: Cayuga Press, 1939 (pp. 11-18). Also appears in The College Years, edited by A. C. Spectorsky. New York: Hawthorn Books, 1958 (pp. 464-67).

"Introduction" to A Basic Chicken Guide for the Small Flock Owner by Roy Edwin Jones. New York: William Morrow, 1944.

"Introduction" to The Lives and Times of Archy and Mehitabel by Don Marquis. Garden City, N.Y.: Doubleday, 1950.

"Introduction" to Spider, Egg, and Microcosm: Three Men and Three Worlds of Science by Eugene Kinkead. New York: Alfred A. Knopf, 1955.

"Introduction and Notes" to Walden by Henry David Thoreau. Boston: Houghton Mifflin, 1964.

"A Teaching Trinity" in The Teacher, edited by Morris L. Ernst. Englewood Cliffs, N.J.: Prentice-Hall, 1967 (pp. 103-105).

"Introduction" to "Reader's Report: A Selected List of Books by Morris Bishop, Professor Emeritus of Cornell University, with Notes and Comments by Some of His Friends and Colleagues." Cornell University: John M. Olin Library, Bookmark Series, Special Number 46, April 15, 1971 (pp. [1]-[2]).

MISCELLANEOUS

"Personal Column," The Seattle Daily Times. From March 7 to June 20, 1923, White maintained a "Personal Column," which consisted of poems, paragraphs, and observations of various sorts.

March 7, 1923, pp. 1, 2.
March 8, 1923, pp. 1, 2.
March 9, 1923, p. 2.
March 10, 1923, p. 2.
March 12, 1923, p. 2.
March 13, 1923, p. 2.
March 14, 1923, p. 5.
March 15, 1923, p. 7.
March 16, 1923, p. 11.
March 17, 1923, p. 2.
March 19, 1923, p. 4.
March 20, 1923, p. 10.
March 21, 1923, p. 8
March 22, 1923, p. 8
March 23, 1923, p. 15.
March 24, 1923, p. 2.
March 26, 1923, p. 9.
March 27, 1923, p. 9.
March 28, 1923, p. 16.
March 29, 1923, p. 12.
March 30, 1923, p. 10.
March 31, 1923, p. 3.
April 2, 1923, p. 9.
April 3, 1923, p. 10.
April 4, 1923, p. 21.
April 5, 1923, p. 16.
April 6, 1923, p. 13.
April 7, 1923, p. 3.
April 9, 1923, p. 10.
April 10, 1923, p. 12.
April 11, 1923, p. 10.
April 12, 1923, p. 11.
April 13, 1923, p. 20.
April 14, 1923, p. 9.
April 16, 1923, p. 10.
April 18, 1923, p. 13.
April 19, 1923, p. 16.
April 20, 1923, p. 19.
April 21, 1923, p. 3.
April 23, 1923, p. 7.
April 24, 1923, p. 2.
April 25, 1923, p. 13.
April 26, 1923, p. 13.
April 27, 1923, p. 23.
April 28, 1923, p. 2.
April 30, 1923, p. 17.
May 1, 1923, p. 9.
May 2, 1923, p. 9.
May 3, 1923, p. 13.
May 4, 1923, p. 13.
May 5, 1923, p. 2.
May 7, 1923, p. 12.
May 8, 1923, p. 10.
May 9, 1923, p. 16.
May 10, 1923, p. 14.
May 11, 1923, p. 22.
May 12, 1923, p. 2.
May 14, 1923, p. 7.
May 15, 1923, p. 9.
May 16, 1923, p. 19.

May 17, 1923, p. 16.
May 18, 1923, p. 14.
May 19, 1923, p. 3.
May 21, 1923, p. 4.
May 22, 1923, p. 14.
May 23, 1923, p. 5.
May 24, 1923, p. 15.
May 25, 1923, p. 7.
May 26, 1923, p. 4.
May 28, 1923, p. 11.
May 29, 1923 p. 10.
May 30, 1923, p. 12.
May 21, 1923, p. 16.
June 1, 1923, p. 8.
June 2, 1923, p. 9.
June 4, 1923, p. 18.
June 5, 1923, p. 10.
June 6, 1923, p. 7.
June 7, 1923, p. 11.
June 8, 1923, p. 4.
June 9, 1923, p. 2.
June 11, 1923, p. 11.
June 12, 1923, p. 12.
June 13, 1923, p. 17.
June 14, 1923, p. 10.
June 15, 1923, p. 15.
June 16, 1923, p. 2.
June 18, 1923, p. 2.
June 19, 1923, p. 12.
June 20, 1923, p. 10.

"Answers to Hard Questions," The New Yorker. In which White reacts to a question, comment, observation or the like that appeared in print somewhere with an answer, comment or observation of his own.

Volume V, July 6, 1929, p. 15.
Volume VIII, April 16, 1932, p. 25.
Volume X, November 17, 1934, p. 63.
Volume XI, December 7, 1935, p. 77.
Volume XIII, May 9, 1936, p. 84.
  August 29, 1936, p. 39.
  September 12, 1936, p. 53.
Volume XIV, July 16, 1938, p. 46.
  July 23, 1938, pp. 49-50.
  August 13, 1938, p. 52.
  January 14, 1939, p. 48.
Volume XV, February 25, 1939, p. 59.
  March 11, 1939, p. 56.
  March 25, 1939, p. 88.
  June 10, 1939, p. 63.
  September 30, 1939, p. 61.
Volume XVI, March 16, 1940, p. 81.
  April 13, 1940, p. 79.
  September 7, 1940, p. 30.
  November 9, 1940, p. 50.
Volume XVII, November 22, 1941, p. 44.
Volume XVIII, February 21, 1942, p. 19.
  March 28, 1942, p. 36.
  April 11, 1942, p. 30
  October 10, 1942, p. 32.
  November 14, 1942, p. 38.

Volume XIX, June 5, 1943, p. 77.
November 20, 1943, p. 100.
Volume XX, May 13, 1944, p. 70.
June 24, 1944, p. 80.
Volume XXI, June 9, 1945, p. 68.
July 21, 1945, p. 42.
Volume XXIII, March 15, 1947, p. 93.
April 19, 1947, p. 102.
Volume XXIV, November 20, 1948, p. 61.
December 18, 1948, p. 102.
Volume XXV, May 14, 1949, p. 104.
June 11, 1949, p. 58.
August 20, 1949, p. 49.
October 1, 1949, p. 51.
Volume XXVI, February 25, 1950, p. 112.
Volume XXIX, January 9, 1954, p. 59.
January 23, 1954, p. 61.
Volume XXXI, March 26, 1955, p. 93.
October 1, 1955, p. 113.
November 26, 1955, p. 144.
Volume XXXII, October 13, 1956, p. 180.
Volume XXXIII, February 23, 1957, p. 118.
December 21, 1957, p. 38.
Volume XXXIV, July 5, 1958, p. 64.
October 11, 1958, p. 84.
November 8, 1958, p. 183.
Volume XXXV, June 27, 1959, p. 82.
Volume XXXVIII, April 14, 1962, p. 177.
October 20, 1962, p. 217.
February 16, 1963, p. 149.
Volume XXXIX, July 27, 1963, p. 77.
August 17, 1963, p. 66.
December 7, 1963, p. 248.
Volume XL, August 8, 1964, p. 73.
September 26, 1964, p. 163.
Volume XLI, October 30, 1965, p. 107.
Volume XLII, November 12, 1966, p. 193.
Volume XLIII, June 3, 1967, p. 148.
Volume XLIV, November 30, 1968, p. 198.
Volume XLV, June 28, 1969, p. 82.
October 4, 1969, p. 160.
Volume XLVII, February 12, 1972, p. 67.
Volume XLVIII, March 4, 1972, p. 86.
September 23, 1972, p. 73.
September 30, 1972, p. 121.
Volume XLIX, November 5, 1973, p. 142.
January 21, 1974, p. 71.
February 18, 1974, p. 91.

Volume LI, March 10, 1975, p. 87.
Volume LII, August 9, 1975, p. 63.

"These Precious Days," The New Yorker. This series is subtitled "The New Yorker's fever chart of planet Earth, showing Man's ups and downs in contaminating the air, the sea, and the soil." It consists of a collection of "bulletins tracing Man's progress in making the planet uninhabitable."

Volume XXXV, May 16, 1959, pp. 168-169.
May 23, 1959, pp. 137-138.
June 6, 1959, pp. 147-148.
June 20, 1959, pp. 92, 95.
July 11, 1959, pp. 67-68.
July 25, 1959, pp. 65-66.
August 22, 1959, p. 91.
August 29, 1959, pp. 66-67.
October 3, 1959, pp. 135-136.
October 31, 1959, pp. 175-176.
November 14, 1959, p. 208.
December 12, 1959, pp. 194-195.
December 19, 1959, pp. 121-122.
January 30, 1960, pp. 73-74, 76.
Volume XXXVI, March 5, 1960, pp. 132-134.
April 2, 1960, pp. 95-96.
April 30, 1960, pp. 109-110.

Obituaries, The New Yorker. Unless otherwise noted, these obituary notices are unsigned.

"Send-off: Frannie J. Reed," V (July 27, 1929), 8-9.

"Notes and Comment: Ring Lardner," IX (October 7, 1933), 11.

"Notes and Comment: Frank Perry," X (August 11, 1934), 7.

"Notes and Comment: James Hannon," X (November 10, 1934), 13.

"Clarence Day," XI (January 11, 1936), 10.

"Notes and Comment: Alexander Woollcott," XVIII (January 30, 1943), 9-10.

"Notes and Comment: Franklin Delano Roosevelt," XXI (April 21, 1945), 17-18.

"Helen E. Hopkinson," XXV (November 12, 1949), 160.

"Notes and Comment: Charles G. Ross," XXVI (December 16, 1950), 23.

"Alva Johnston," XXVI (December 23, 1950), 39. (Signed "The Editors.")

"H. W. Ross," XXVII (December 15, 1951), 23.

"G. S. Lobrano," XXXII (March 10, 1956), 155.

"Wolcott Gibbs," XXXIV (August 30, 1958), 83.

"Notes and Comment: F.P.A.," XXXVI (April 2, 1960), 31.

"James Thurber," XXXVII (November 11, 1961), 247. (White wrote the second half of this obituary.)

"Notes and Comment: John Fitzgerald Kennedy," XXXIX (November 30, 1963), 49-50.

Other Miscellaneous Writings:

"Sterling Finny Advertisements," The New Yorker. From April 9, to July 2, 1927, White wrote a series of advertisements, which ran in The New Yorker in the early years when the magazine was trying to promote its circulation.

Volume III, April 9, 1927, p. 61: "Darling he bought everybody a soda but me!"

April 16, 1927, p. 112: "Good morning, stupid!"

April 23, 1927, p. 8: "Our little son must never know."

April 30, 1927, p. 49: "You are a saintly woman--and that about covers it!"

May 7, 1927, p. 6: "This is capital fun for me!"

May 28, 1927, p. 47: "They giggled when he stirred the soup with his finger."

June 4, 1927, p. 92: "He was never more boring than when he was sleeping."

June 18, 1927, p. 91: "They wondered why the caddy walked away."

June 25, 1927, p. 45: "She married me for my muscular system."

July 2, 1927, p. 71: "Even the horse was sick of the whole business!"

Letters to the Editor:

"Letter to the Editor," The New York Times, July 9, 1942, p. 19.

"Letter to the Editor: The Age of Fear--Mr. White Thinks We Fell Over the Cat," The New York Herald Tribune, December 2, 1947, p. 30.

"Letter to the Editor: These Edgy Times--Mr. White Believes Us Needlessly Unkind," The New York Herald Tribune, December 9, 1947, p. 34.

"Letter to the Editor," The New York Times, April 17, 1949, VI, p. 30.

"Trade Winds: Reply," Saturday Review, XXXVI (January 3, 1953), 6.

Plays:

White wrote a play, entitled "The Firebug's Homecoming," which is in typescript (12 pages) and is available only at the General Library and Museum of the Performing Arts division of the New York Public Library at Lincoln Center. The original copy at the Lincoln Center Library bears this notation: "Revised May 18th, 1932."

Cartoons:

White wrote the caption to the famous Carl Rose "spinach" cartoon, which appears in The New Yorker, IV, December 8, 1928, p. 27.

Maine Lobsterman Script:

White wrote the script for a documentary television film on Maine Lobstermen that was made by "Omnibus" and broadcast on December 5, 1954.

Right of Privacy Speech:

White wrote a speech, entitled "The Right of Privacy," which was recorded at WLBZ in Bangor, Maine, July 1, 1961, for the "Voice of America."

New Yorker Cover

The April 23, 1932, *New Yorker* had a sea-green cover, featuring seahorses, drawn by White. This is the only cover he did for the magazine.

Part II

Writings about E. B. White

BIOGRAPHY AND CRITICISM

Ingersoll, Ralph. "The New Yorker," Fortune, X (August, 1934), 72-86, 90, 92, 97, 150, 152.

Thurber, James. "E. B. W.," The Saturday Review, XVIII (October 15, 1938), 8-9. Reprinted in Essay Annual, 1939, pp. 9-14 and The Saturday Review Gallery, 1959, pp. 302-307.

Alsterlund, B. "E. B. White," Wilson Library Bulletin, XIII (January, 1939), 298.

Bacon, Leonard. "Humors and Careers," The Saturday Review, XX (April 29, 1939), 3-4, 22.

van Gelder, Robert. "An Interview with Mr. E. B. White, Essayist," The New York Times Book Review, August 2, 1942, p. 2. Reprinted in a collection of van Gelder's interviews, Writers and Writing, 1946, pp. 308-310.

Kunitz, Stanley J., ed. Twentieth Century Authors. New York: H. W. Wilson, 1942, p. 1508.

"Books and Authors," The New York Times, May 23, 1945, p. 17.

Adams, J. Donald. "Speaking of Books," The New York Times Book Review, June 3, 1945, p. 2.

Fadiman, Clifton. "In Praise of E. B. White, Realist," The New York Times Book Review, June 10, 1945, pp. 1, 10, 12, 14-16. An abridged version is included in Party of One: The Selected Writings of Clifton Fadiman, 1955, under the title "A Traveler in Reality," pp. 54-62.

Beck, Warren. "E. B. White," The English Journal, XXXV (April, 1946), 175-181.

Maloney, Russell. "Tilley the Toiler: A Profile of the New Yorker Magazine," The Saturday Review, XXX (August 30, 1947), 7-10, 29-32.

"Go Climb a More Meaningful Tree," The Commonweal, LI (March 10, 1950), 573.

Kramer, Dale. Ross and the New Yorker. New York: Doubleday, 1951.

Nulton, Lucy. "Eight-Year-Olds Tangled in 'Charlotte's Web'," Elementary English, XXXI (January, 1954), 11-16.

Breit, Harvey. "In and Out of Books," The New York Times Book Review, January 17, 1954, p. 8.

Fenton, John H. "Kirk, at Harvard, Asks Free Inquiry," The New York Times, June 18, 1954, p. 20.

Kunitz, Stanley J., ed. Twentieth Century Authors. 1st suppl. New York: H. W. Wilson, 1955, p. 1072.

Fuller, John Wesley. Prose Styles in the Essays of E. B. White. Seattle: University of Washington, 1959.

Thurber, James. The Years with Ross. Boston: Little, Brown, 1959.

Moritz, Charles, ed. Current Biography Yearbook. New York: H. W. Wilson, 1960, pp. 453-455.

"Typewriter Man," Newsweek, February 22, 1960, p. 72.

Nordell, Roderick. "The Writer as Private Man," The Christian Science Monitor, October 31, 1962, p. 9.

Steinhoff, William R. "'The Door,' 'The Professor,' 'My Friend the Poet (Deceased),' 'The Washable House,' and 'The Man Out in Jersey'," College English, XXIII (December, 1961), 229-232.

Weatherby, W. J. "A Modern Man of Walden," Manchester Guardian Weekly, February 14, 1963, p. 14.

"Freedom Medal Honors Kennedy," The New York Times, December 7, 1963, pp. 1, 14.

Frank, Susan I. "E. B. White Recalls Cornell Years," The Cornell Daily Sun, October 9, 1964, pp. S2, S8.

______. "White Enjoys Relaxed Climate with Picturesque View of Bay," The Cornell Daily Sun, October 9, 1964, p. S2.

Yates, Norris W. "E. B. White, 'Farmer/Other'," The American Humorist: Conscience of the Twentieth Century, rev. 2nd printing. Ames: Iowa State University Press, 1964, pp. 299-320.

Benet, Laura. Famous English and American Essayists. New York: Dodd, Mead, 1966, pp. 119-122.

Grant, Jane. Ross, the New Yorker and Me. New York: Reynal, 1968.

Shenker, Israel. "E. B. White: Notes and Comment by Author," The New York Times, July 11, 1969, pp. 31, 43.

Plimpton, George A., and Frank H. Crowther. "The Art of the Essay. I. E. B. White," The Paris Review, XLVIII (Fall, 1969), 65-88.

Smaridge, Norah. Famous Modern Storytellers for Young People. New York: Dodd, Mead, 1969.

Raymont, Henry. "Children's Books Reward Authors," The New York Times, January 23, 1970, p. 45.

Weales, Gerald. "The Designs of E. B. White," The New York Times Children's Book Review, May 24, 1970, pp. 2, 10.

Ellege, Scott. "Andy White at Cornell," Cornell Alumni News, April, 1971, pp. 19-23.

Hasley, Louis. "The Talk of the Town and Country: E. B. White," Connecticut Review, V (October, 1971), 37-45.

Nordstrom, Ursula. "Stuart, Wilbur, Charlotte: A Tale of Tales," The New York Times Book Review, May 12, 1974, pp. 98-99.

Crowley, James G. "In Quest of E. B. White," Boston Globe Magazine, June 30, 1974, pp. 4, 6-7.

Hopkins, Lee Bennett. More Books by More People: Interviews with Sixty-Five Authors of Books for Children. New York: Citation Press, 1974, pp. 375-381.

Sampson, Edward C. E. B. White. New York: Twayne Publishers, 1974. (Twayne's United States Author Series, no. 232.)

Wintle, Justin and Emma Fisher. The Pied Pipers: Interviews with the Influential Creators of Children's Literature. New York: Paddington Press, 1974, pp. 124-131.

Scriba, Jay. "E. B. White," Biography News, II (November/December, 1975), 1354.

Gill, Brendan. Here at the New Yorker. New York: Random House, 1975.

Franks, Lucinda. "E. B. White Takes on Xerox and Wins," The New York Times, June 15, 1976, pp. 1, 74.

"Saving the Free Press," National Review, XXVIII (July 9, 1976), 721.

Mitgang, Herbert. "Down East with E. B. White," The New York Times, Sec. 3, November 17, 1976, p. 19.

"E. B. White: A Man of Letters," Publishers Weekly, (December 13, 1976), pp. 42-43.

Updike, John. "Remarks," Picked-Up Pieces. New York: Alfred A. Knopf, 1976, pp. 434-437.

Mitgang, Herbert. "Behind the Best Sellers: E. B. White," The New York Times Book Review, November 20, 1977, p. 68.

REVIEWS OF E. B. WHITE'S BOOKS

IS SEX NECESSARY? OR, WHY YOU FEEL THE WAY YOU DO

Dodd, Lee Wilson. "A Monograph with Punch," The Saturday Review of Literature, VI (December 7, 1929), 506.

Cuppy, Will. "Bluebirds and What Not," New York Herald Tribune Books, December 8, 1929, p. 5.

Henson, Harry. The New York World, December 20, 1929, p. 14.

THE LADY IS COLD

Walton, Eda Lou. "Light Verse," New York Herald Tribune Books, May 26, 1929, p. 6.

Hicks, Granville. The New York World, June 23, 1929, p. 7M.

Boston Evening Transcript Book Section, July 6, 1929, p. 4.

The Nation, CXXIX (August 14, 1929), 177.

Bookman, LXX (October, 1929), xvi.

EVERY DAY IS SATURDAY

Brickell, Herschel. The New York Post, October 6, 1934, p. 7.

The New York Times Book Review, October 7, 1934, p. 9.

"Thoreau on a Roof Garden," New York Herald Tribune Books, October 14, 1934, p. 23.

Boston Evening Transcript Book Section, October 20, 1934, p. 2.

Benet, William Rose. "For Future Historians," The Saturday Review of Literature, XI (October 27, 1934), 240.

The Booklist, XXXI (December, 1934), 124.

FAREWELL TO MODEL T

The New York Times Book Review, October 11, 1936, p. 10.

Boston Evening Transcript Book Section, October 31, 1936, p. 9.

The Christian Science Monitor Weekly Magazine Section, November 18, 1936, p. [14]

THE FOX OF PEAPACK AND OTHER POEMS

"Likes and Dislikes," Time XXXII (October 10, 1938), 68.

The New Yorker, XIV (October 15, 1938), 72.

The Booklist, XXXV (November 1, 1938), 81.

The Saturday Review of Literature, XIX (November 12, 1938), 20.

McCord, David. "Lightest of the Arts," Yale Review, XXVIII (December, 1938), 393-394.

QUO VADIMUS?
OR, THE CASE FOR THE BICYCLE

The New Yorker, XV (March 4, 1939), 80.

Cuppy, Will. "Master of Sense and Sentences," New York Herald Tribune Books, March 5, 1939, p. 2.

Sherman, Beatrice. "Drifting Whither with E. B. White,"

The New York Times Book Review, March 5, 1939, p. 3.

"Humorist," Time, XXXIII (March 6, 1939), 61.

The Springfield Republican, March 7, 1939, p. 8.

"Case for the Quo," The Christian Science Monitor, March 17, 1939, p. 20.

Edman, Irwin. "1000 Reasons, All Good," The Saturday Review of Literature, XIX (March 18, 1939), 7.

Boston Evening Transcript Book Reviews, March 25, 1939, p. 2.

Wisconsin Library Bulletin, XXXV (April, 1939), 62.

The Booklist, XXXV (April 1, 1939), 249.

Ferguson, Otis. "No Hands," The New Republic, IC (June 20, 1939), 226-227.

A SUBTREASURY OF AMERICAN HUMOR

Fadiman, Clifton. The New Yorker, XVII (November 8, 1941), 91.

Adams, J. Donald. "Speaking of Books," The New York Times Book Review, November 9, 1941, p. 2.

The Springfield Republican, November 15, 1941, p. 6.

Walker, Stanley. "Anthology of Laughter," New York Herald Tribune Books, November 16, 1941, p. 6.

Bacon, Leonard. "How to Break a Rib," The Saturday Review, XXIV (November 22, 1941), 7-8.

Weeks, Edward. The Atlantic Monthly, CLXVIII (December, 1941), [814].

Wisconsin Library Bulletin, XXXVII (December, 1941), 199.

The Booklist, XXXVIII (December 1, 1941), 110.

Ferguson, Otis. "Laughter, Not Immoderate," The New Republic, CV (December 15, 1941), 832.

The Catholic World, CLIV (January, 1942), 509-510.

Wyatt, E. V. R. The Commonweal, XXXV (January 2, 1942), 273-274.

ONE MAN'S MEAT

The New Yorker, XVIII (June 13, 1942), 72.

Canby, Henry S. "... But No Man's Poison," The Saturday Review, XXV (June 13, 1942), 7.

Edman, Irwin. "Earthy, Humorous, Accessible," New York Herald Tribune Books, June 14, 1942, p. 2.

Feld, Rose. "E. B. White Surveys His World," The New York Times Book Review, June 14, 1942, p. 8.

"Last Look Around," Time, XXXIX (June 22, 1942), 91-92.

Weeks, Edward. "First Person Singular," The Atlantic Monthly, CLXX (July, 1942), 100.

Wisconsin Library Bulletin, XXXVIII (July, 1942), 118.

The Booklist, XXXVIII (July 15, 1942), 438.

Hyman, Stanley E. "The Urban New Yorker," The New Republic, CVII (July 20, 1942), 90-92.

Catholic World, CLV (August, 1942), 627-628.

Trilling, Diana. "Humanity and Humor," The Nation, CLV (August 8, 1942), 118.

De Vane, William C. "A Celebration of Life," Yale Review, XXXII (Autumn, 1942), 163-165.

Ellege, Scott. "One Man's Meat by E. B. White," The Carleton Miscellany, IV (Winter, 1964), 83-87.

Publishers Weekly, February 14, 1966, p. 146.

STUART LITTLE

Kirkus, XIII (July 15, 1945), 314.

Becker, May Lamberton. New York Herald Tribune Weekly Book Review, October 21, 1945, p. 6.

The Springfield Republican, October 21, 1945, p. 4d.

Chicago Sun Book Week, October 28, 1945, p. 2.

Cowley, Malcolm. "Stuart Little: Or New York Through the Eyes of a Mouse," The New York Times Book Review, October 28, 1945, 7.

Horn Book, XXI (November, 1945), 455.

Wisconsin Library Bulletin, XLI (December, 1945), 129.

White, K. S. "Children's Books: Fairy Tales and the Postwar World," The New Yorker, XXI (December 8, 1945), 120.

Benet, Rosemary Carr. "Mrs. Little's Second Son," The Saturday Review of Literature, XXVIII (December 8, 1945), 26.

Binsse, Harry Lorin. The Commonweal, XLIII (December 28, 1945), 294.

"Mouse & Moujik," Time, XXXXVI (December 31, 1945), 92-94.

Publishers Weekly, January 23, 1967, p. 262.

THE WILD FLAG: EDITORIALS FROM THE NEW YORKER ON FEDERAL WORLD GOVERNMENT AND OTHER MATTERS

Kirkus, XIV (August 15, 1946), 403.

Willis, Katherine Tappert. Library Journal, LXXI (October 1, 1946), 1330.

Watson, Mark S. "Mr. White Surveys the World," The Saturday Review of Literature, XXIX (November 9, 1946), 14-15.

Edman, Irwin. "E. B. White, That Fine Goldsmith in Words," New York Herald Tribune Weekly Book Review, November 10, 1946, p. 5.

"Brave New Scanties," Time, XXXXVIII (November 11, 1946), 109-110.

Poore, Charles. "Pointers for Statesman or Skeptic," The New York Times Book Review, November 17, 1946, p. 3, 58.

The Booklist, XLIII (December 1, 1946), 96.

Jackson, J. H. The San Francisco Chronicle, December 3, 1946, p. 16.

Beck, Warren. The Chicago Sun Book Week, December 15, 1946, p. 3.

"One Flag for One World," The Christian Science Monitor Magazine Section, December 21, 1946, p. 11.

Rosenfeld, Isaac. "Chopping a Teakettle," The Nation, CLXIII (December 28, 1946), 762-763.

Weeks, Edward. "The Peripatetic Reviewer," The Atlantic Monthly, CLXXIX (January, 1947), 106.

Current History, XII (January, 1947), 60.

HERE IS NEW YORK

Kirkus, XVII (September 15, 1949), 532.

The New Yorker, XXV (December 17, 1949), 120, 123.

Berger, Meyer. "Crystal-Clear New York," The New York Times Book Review, December 18, 1949, p. 7.

Jackson, J. H. The San Francisco Chronicle, December 21, 1949, p. 18.

The Springfield Republican, January 8, 1950, p. 17A.

Saturday Review of Literature, XXXIII (January 14, 1950), 36.

Kiniery, Paul. Best Sellers, IX (January 15, 1950), 168.

Sugrue, Thomas. "Love Letter to Manhattan," New York Herald Tribune Book Review, January 22, 1950, p. 3.

CHARLOTTE'S WEB

Kirkus, XX (August 15, 1952), 501.

The Booklist, XLIX (September 1, 1952), 2.

Welty, Eudora. "Life in the Barn Was Very Good," The New York Times Book Review, October 19, 1952, p. 49.

Cerf, Bennett. "Trade Winds," The Saturday Review, XXXV (November 15, 1952), 6-7.

The Chicago Sunday Tribune, November 16, 1952, p. 4.

Travers, P. L. "Tangible Magic," New York Herald Tribune Book Review, Pt. II, November 16, 1952, pp. 1, 38.

The Times Literary Supplement (London), November 28, 1952, p. 7.

Travers, P. L. "My Childhood Bends Beside Me," The New Statesman and Nation, XXXXIV (November 29, 1952), 639.

The Springfield Republican, November 30, 1952, p. 7C.

Weeks, Edward. "The Peripatetic Reviewer," The Atlantic Monthly, CXC (December, 1952), 88, 90.

Kieran, Margaret Ford. The Atlantic Monthly, CXC (December, 1952), 101.

Moore, Anne Carroll. "The Three Owl's Notebook," Horn Book XXVIII (December, 1952), 394.

Lindquist, Jennie D. Horn Book, XXVIII (December, 1952), 407-408.

Kinkead, Katharine T. The New Yorker, XXVIII (December 6, 1952), 194.

Hodges, Elizabeth. Library Journal, LXXVII (December 15, 1952), 2185-2186.

Publishers Weekly, January 23, 1967, p. 262.

Kight, Margie. Catholic Library World, XXXVIII (March, 1967), 474.

Gray, Geraldine. New Catholic World, CCXVI (March-April, 1973), 92.

Van Horne, Geneva P., and Carol Nauth Euller, Instructor, LXXXIV (November, 1974), 142.

THE SECOND TREE FROM THE CORNER

Kirkus, XXI (November 1, 1953), 725.

The Booklist, L (December 15, 1953), 157.

Barron, Louis. Library Journal, LXXIX (January 15, 1954), 142.

Beck, Warren. The Chicago Sunday Tribune, January 17, 1954, p. 5.

Sherwood, Robert E. "E. B. White: A Treasury of That Modest, Wise and Witty Master," New York Herald Tribune Book Review, January 17, 1954, pp. 1, 13.

Edman, Irwin. "The Wonder and Wackiness of Man," The New York Times Book Review, January 17, 1954, p. 1.

"Tidbits & Pieces," Time, LXIII (January 25, 1954), 116-117.

Krutch, Joseph Wood. "The Profession of a New Yorker," Saturday Review, XXXVIII (June 30, 1954), 15-16.

The Bookmark, XIII (February, 1954), 107.

Jackson, J. H. The San Francisco Chronicle, February 3, 1954, p. 15.

Webster, Harvey Curtis, "Sense and Style," New Republic, CXXX (February 15, 1954), 19.

Weeks, Edward. The Peripatetic Reviewer," Atlantic Monthly, CXCIII (March, 1954), 76, 78.

Wisconsin Library Bulletin, L (March, 1954), 68.

"Humorist with a Heart," The Times Literary Supplement (London), April 9, 1954, p. 234.

"Analysing Humour," The Manchester Guardian, May 7, 1954, p. 6.

The Nation, CLXXVIII (May 29, 1954), 469.

United States Quarterly Book Review, X (June, 1964), 186.

THE ELEMENTS OF STYLE

Hogan, William. The San Francisco Chronicle, May 22, 1959, p. 35.

"Rules for Good Writing," The Christian Science Monitor, May 28, 1959, p. 11.

The Booklist, LV (June 15, 1959), 572.

Barrett, Mary L. Library Journal, LXXXIV (June 15, 1959), 2068.

The New Yorker, XXXV (June 20, 1959), 111.

Wisconsin Library Bulletin, LV (July, 1959), 370.

"'Elements of Style' in Revised Edition," The Springfield Republican, July 19, 1959, p. 4D.

Hicks, Granville, "Clarity, Clarity, Clarity," Saturday Review, XXXXII (August 1, 1959), 13.

Christian Century, LXXVI (August 26, 1959), 973.

The New Yorker, XXXXVIII (June 24, 1972), 95.

Cosgrave, Mary Silva. Horn Book, XLVIII (October, 1972), 496.

THE POINTS OF MY COMPASS

Kirkus, XXX (August 1, 1962), 746.

Hogan, William. The San Francisco Chronicle, October 12, 1962, p. 37.

Nordell, Roderick. "'The Safekeeping of ... Enchantment'," The Christian Science Monitor, October 18, 1962, p. 9.

Fuller, Edmund. "Multitude of Topics Touched by a True Master of Style," Chicago Sunday Tribune Magazine of Books, October 21, 1962, p. 2.

Walker, Stanley. "E. B. White's Civilized Way of Saying Things," New York Herald Tribune, October 21, 1962, p. 5.

Arlen, M. J. "World of E. B. White," The New York Book Review, October 28, 1962, p. 24.

The Booklist, LIX (November 15, 1962), 238.

Schott, Webster. "E. B. White Forever," The New Republic, CXLVII (November 24, 1962), 23-24.

Gold, Herbert. "'The Points of My Compass: Letters from the East, the West, the North, the South,' by E. B. White," Saturday Review, XLV (November 24, 1962), 30.

Barrett, William. "Reader's Choice," The Atlantic Monthly, CCX (December, 1962), 172.

AN E. B. WHITE READER

The Booklist, LXII (May 1, 1966), 860.

Library Journal, IXC (May 15, 1966), 2725.

Choice, III (November, 1966), 774.

THE TRUMPET OF THE SWAN

Kirkus, XXXVIII (April 15, 1970), 455.

Publishers Weekly, April 20, 1970, 62.

Goodwin, Polly. *The Chicago Sunday Tribune Children's Book World*, May 17, 1970, pp. 4-5.

Sutherland, Zena. *Saturday Review*, LIII (June 27, 1970), 39.

Updike, John. *The New York Times Book Review*, June 28, 1970, pp. 4-5, 24.

Fuller, Edmund. "E. B. White's Tale of Swans and Children Delights & Instructs," *The Wall Street Journal*, July 14, 1970, p. 16.

"Another Louis Takes Up the Horn," *The Christian Science Monitor*, July 25, 1970, p. 15.

Heins, Paul. *Horn Book*, XVIL (August, 1970), 391.

"Mr. White's 'Trumpet of the Swan' Is an Elegiac If One-Key Pastorale," *The National Observer*, August 10, 1970, p. 21.

Agree, Rose H. *Instructor*, LXXX (August/September, 1970), p. 173.

Weeks, Edward. "The Peripatetic Reviewer," *The Atlantic Monthly*, CCXXVI (September, 1970), 123-124.

The Booklist, LXVI (September 1, 1970), 59.

Bulletin of the Center for Children's Books, XXIV (October, 1970), 35-36.

Wilson, Hazel. *Parent's Magazine*, VL (October, 1970), 20.

Kellman, Amy. *Grade Teacher*, LXXXVIII (November, 1970), 120.

America, CXXIII (December 5, 1970), 496.

Stafford, Jean. *The New Yorker*, XXXXVI (December 5, 1970), 217-218.

The New York Times Book Review, December 6, 1970, p. 58.

The Times Literary Supplement (London), December 11, 1970, p. 1458.

Library Journal, VC (December 15, 1970), 4327.

Hentoff, Margot. _The New York Review of Books_, XV (December 17, 1970), 11.

Time, IVC (December 21, 1970), 68.

Howard, Janet. _Childhood Education_, XVIIL (February, 1971), 265.

Higgins, Judith. _Teacher_, LXXXXI (May/June, 1974), 81-82.

LETTERS OF E. B. WHITE

Kirkus Reviews, XXXXIV (September 15, 1976), 1078.

Marvin, John R. _Library Journal_, CI (October 1, 1976), 2057.

Publishers Weekly, October 18, 1976, p. 54.

Booklist, LXXIII (November 15, 1976), 446.

McPherson, William. "The White Papers: First Class Mail," _The Washington Post Book World_, November 21, 1976, p. E1.

Sheed, Wilfred. _The New York Times Book Review_, November 21, 1976, pp. 1, 26, 28.

Weales, Gerald. "Writer at Large," _The Nation_, CCXXIII (December 4, 1976), 597-599.

The Washington Post Book World, December 5, 1976, p. H6.

Broyard, Anatole. "Seriously Un-Serious," _The New York Times_, December 7, 1976, p. 39.

Stafford, Jean. "A Green Thumb in a Mass of Clenched Fists," _Saturday Review_, IV (December 11, 1976), 61-63.

Davis, L. J. "Is Prose Dead? Not to E. B. White," The National Observer, December 18, 1976, p. 19.

Kanfer, Stefan. Time, LXXIV (December 20, 1976), 74-75.

Breslin, John B. America, CXXXV (December 25, 1976), 471-472.

Updike, John. "Of Beauty and Consternation," The New Yorker, LII (December 27, 1976), 64-68.

Nordell, Roderick. "White's Letters: The Lofty with the Mundane," The Christian Science Monitor, January 5, 1977, p. 23.

O'Connell, Shaun. "E. B. White Letters Provide a Constant Delight," The Boston Sunday Globe, January 9, 1977, p. 100.

Fuller, Edmund. "The Public Force of a Private Man," The Wall Street Journal, January 17, 1977, p. 14.

Muggeridge, Malcolm. "The Compleat New Yorker," Harper's, CCLIV (March, 1977), 94, 98-99.

Yardley, Jonathan. "E. B. White ... Greatness in Miniature," The Pittsburgh Press Family Magazine, March 6, 1977, p. 4.

Cosgrave, Mary Silva. Horn Book, LIII (April, 1977), 201.

Choice, XIV (April, 1977), 206.

Brown, Spencer. "White of the Rueful Countenance," The American Scholar, XXXXVI (Spring, 1977), 237-240, 254.

Core, George. "A Mask and an Unveiling," The Sewanee Review, LXXXV (Spring, 1977), lix-lx.

Stenersen, Stanley G. Journalism Quarterly, LIV (Spring, 1977), 182-183.

Homer, Frank X. J. America, CXXXVI (May 7, 1977), 430.

Hall, Donald. "E. B. White on the Exercycle," National Review, XXIX (June 10, 1977), 671-672.

ESSAYS OF E. B. WHITE

Bach, Bert C. Library Journal, CII (July, 1977), 1499.

Booklist, LXXIII (July 1, 1977), 1621.

Publishers Weekly, July 11, 1977, p. 68.

Kirkus, XXXXV (July 15, 1977), 777.

DeMott, Benjamin. Saturday Review, IV (August 20, 1977), 63.

Welty, Eudora. "Dateless Virtues," The New York Times Book Review, September 25, 1977, pp. 7, 43.

Dennis, Nigel. "Smilin' Through," The New York Review of Books, October 27, 1977, pp. 42-43.

Freedman, Richard. "The Quiet Wit of E. B. White," The Washington Post Book World, November 6, 1977, p. E3.

INDEX (Authors and Titles)

Abbott, George 134, 135
ABC of Security 24
Abercrombie's Deep-Tangled Wildwood 23
Abie's Irish Rose 133
About Myself 96
Absentee Voters 127
Account of How He Spent the Day, October 12, 1968 121
Across the Street and into the Grill 108
Activity 131
Adams, J. Donald 147, 153
Adjustment 61
Advanced Course 125
Affidavit in Platitudes 13
A-Fishing Go 39
Africana 133
After All 134
After the Ball 57
Afternoon of an American Boy 102
Agree, Rose H. 161
Aiken, G. L. 135
Air Made Easy 37
Alexander Woolcott 142
Algernon Charles Swinburne, Slightly Cock-eyed, Sees the Old Year Out 12
Alice Through the Cellophane 5
Alice Through the Cellophane: I. Down the Rabbit Hole 63
Alice Through the Cellophane: II. Pool of Tears 63
Alice Through the Cellophane: III. Advice from a Caterpillar 63
Alice, Where Wert Thou? 59
All for Xmas 26
Alma Mater's Eggs 58
Alsterlund, B. 147
Alternatives 11
Alumni Organization 130

Alva Johnston 143
Always 27
America 30
Amiable Nonentity 23
Amor Soporus 9
Analysing Humour 159
And Great Was the Noise Thereof 127
And If One Had a Kennel One Might Call It a Dog Den So That It Might Remind One of Ogden 15, 16
And Jake Begat John ... 129
And the Answer Is 130
Anderson, Doris 134
Andrew A. Freeman 54
Andy White at Cornell 149
Animal Voices 48
Ann Vickers 135
Annals of Birdwatching: Mr. Forbusch's Friends 121
Announcement 40
Anomaly of the Co-Ed 127
Anonymous [i.e., E. B. White] 48
Anonymous Letter 124
Another Beaux Arts 125
Another Failure 126
Another Ho Hum, More Newsbreaks from "The New Yorker" 5
Another Louis Takes Up the Horn 161
Another Recruit 124
Another Unit 127
Another Vicious Circle 132
Answer Is "No" 24
Answers to Hard Questions 118, 140, 141, 142
Answers to Long Letters Department 52
Anthology of Laughter 153
Anthony, Norman B. 135
Apostrophe in a Pram Rider 16
Apostrophic Notes from the New-World Physics 19
Arlen, M. J. 160
Armistice Day 128
Around the Corner 77
The Art of the Essay. I: E. B. White 149
Artificial Rinks 128
As the Oith Toins 68
Ascension 36
Association Plans 127
Athletic Tax 125
Augury 11
Aunt Poo 88

Baby Mine 133
Baby's First Step 45
Bach, Bert C. 164
Back Debt 128
Back to the Farm 126
Bacon, Leonard 147, 153
Baedeker Jones 42
Baily Hall Game 128
Ball Playing Crowd 126
Ballad of Little Faith 13
Ballad of Lost Standing 19
Ballade of Meaty Inversions 17
Ballyhoo of 1932 135
Band Concert 131
Bantam and I 9
Bare Facts of 1927 133
Barge Life on a Root Canal 49
Barnes Hall Hospitality 130
Barrett, Mary L. 159
Barrett, William 160
Barretts of Wimpole Street 134
Barron, Louis 158
Bashful Majority 125
Basic Chicken Guide for the Small Flock Owner 138
Basis of Rushing 132
Basketball Again 129
Basketball Competition 128
Battle Royal 125
Beautiful Upon a Hill 97
Beauty in Light 49
Beck, Warren 148, 156, 158
Becker, May Lamberton 155
Beds for Boys 128
Beer and the Constitution 126
Before Baby Came 28
Before Breakfast 16
Beginnings 64
Behind the Best Sellers: E. B. White 150
Belated Christmas Card 12
Belford's Dash 83
Belligerent Balloonists 130
Bells into Box 22
Bellum in Medium Bellum 21
Benet, Laura 149
Benet, Rosemary Carr 155
Benét, William Rose 152
Beppo 12

Berger, Meyer 156
Besichtigung 61
Besier, Rudolf 134
Best Years 135
Better Mousetraps 59
Big Pond 134
Binsse, Harry Lorin 155
Bird Lady 41
Bird Walk 71
Birds and a Blackout 88
Birth-Control Hearing 44
Birth of an Adult 81
Bishop, Morris 6, 138
Bishop Is Here 57
Bisson, Alexandre 133
Biting the Hand That Feeds 124
Black Magic 40
Blessed Event--I 74
Blessed Event--II 74
Bloody Laughter 134
Blue Laws 129
Bluebirds and What Not 151
Bok Ballot Ballad 9
Bolstering Up Tradition 126
Bon Voyage 124
Bones 51
Book Review 15, 16, 18
Boston Is Like No Other Place in the World Only More So 23
Bottomland 133
Bowling Green 8, 9, 26
Boy I Knew 85
Bradford, Robert W. 7
Bradley, David 137
Brave New Scanties 156
Breakfast on Quaker Hill 95
Breakfast with Dorothy Thompson 83
Breakfast with Peers 39
Breaking Training 125
Breit, Harvey 148
Breslin, John B. 163
Brickell, Herschel 151
Brief Moment 135
British Guests 125
Bromfield, Louis 23, 137
Bronx Home News 44
Broun, Heywood 134

Brown, Spencer 163
Browning-Off of Pelham Manor 122
Broyard, Anatole 162
Bryant, George 134
Bulgakov 48
Burdens of High Office 25
Business and Education 130
... But No Man's Poison 154
But We Were Born Free 137
Bye Low Baby 36

C. E. Cases 131
C. S. Jones 50
Cage Delivery 45
Canby, Henry S. 154
Caravan 134
Card of Greeting 21
Card of Thanks 23
Care and Feeding of Begonias, or the Manly Art 38
Carroll, Earl 133
Carrousel 19
Carted Stag 56
Case for the Quo 153
Casino, I Love You 45
Celebration of Life 154
Celebrities 32
Century of Controls 90
Century of Progress 68
Cerf, Bennett 157
Chairs in Snow 25
Champs 35
Chance to Forget Prejudice 130
Charles E. Courtney 126
Charles G. Ross 143
Charles Love Durham '99 127
Charlotte's Web 6
Chatterboxes 68
Cheerful Yawner 128
Cheering Section 128
Chemistry 19
Children's Books: Fairy Tales and the Postwar World 155
Children's Books Reward Authors 149
Child's 8
Child's Play 27
Chivalry of Democracy 130
Chopping a Teakettle 156

Christmas Gift 130
Circus 10
City Evening 12
Civics 42
Clarence Day 20, 74, 142
Clarity, Clarity, Clarity 159
Classic Waits for Me 22
Clear All Wires 135
Climax 135
Clinic Joust 11
Clique 58
Clock Store 32
Cold Feet 31
Cold in Stables 134
Cold Weather 90
Coldly, to the Bronze Bust of Holly in Washington Square 10
Colleges and Poets 132
Colonel Woodcock's Caller 16
Color of Mice 39
Commercialized Football 128
Competitive System 126
Compleat New Yorker 163
Complicated Thoughts About a Small Son 16
Connecticut Lad 18
Conning Tower 8, 9, 10, 11, 12, 13, 14, 15, 16, 17, 18, 19, 20
Constitution 131
Constitution Passes 131
Construction 28
Contrib, to His Sweet Master 19
Coon Hunt 87
Copeland, Nick 135
Core, George 163
Cornell Crew Got Stuck in the Grass 126
Cornell-Dartmouth 128
Cornell Daylight Saving 128
Cornell Era 129
Cornell Fabyan 125
Cornell Hospitality 128
Cornell Loses to Harvard 125
Cornell on Beebe 130
Cornell Rows Harvard 126
Cornell Spirit 127
Cornell Victorious 128
Cornell's Guests 130
Cornell's Share 130
Cosgrave, Mary Silva 159, 163

Cotillion Game 130
Council Elections 126, 127
Council's Action 125
County Fairs, Doctors 87
Couple 30
Courtney Memorial 128
Cowley, Malcolm 155
Cows Wit Wings 13
Crack of Doom 64
Crew Send-Off 125, 126
Crib Again 130
Critic 125
Critique 34
Crocus 10
Cross Country 128
Cross Country Championship 129
Crothers, Rachel 135
Crowley, James G. 150
Crowther, Frank H. 149
Crystal-Clear New York 156
Culliman, Ralph 134
Cuppy, Will 151, 152
Custom-Cut 43

Daab, Hyatt 134
Damrosch, Gretchen 134
Danbury Fair 51
Daniel Roars with Laughter 128
Daniel Webster, the Hay Fever and Me 81
Darling He Bought Everybody a Soda but Me 143
Dateless Virtues 164
David Starr Jordan 126
Davis, Elmer 137
Davis, L. J. 163
Daylight Saving 131
Dear Old Stuff 130
Death of a Pig 102
Debate Team 131
Decent Dance 131
Decide Before Vacation 132
Decline of Sport 102
Decoys 56
Defense of the Bronx River 26
Definitions: Clergyman 27
Definitions: Commuter 10
Definitions: Corset 10

Definitions: Critic 10
Definitions: Prude 10
de Forest, Marian 134
De Mille on the Flossy 50
DeMott, Benjamin 164
Dennis, Nigel 164
Department of Amplification 120
Department of Correction, Amplification, and Abuse 79
Deserted Nation 25
Designs of E. B. White 149
Despot's Got to Think of Everything 20
Destructionist 43
De Vane, William C. 154
Dewey, John 136
Dexter S. Kimball 128
Diary for a Week 90
Dietz, Howard 135
Dinner in Virginia 18
Dinner with Henry Luce 86
Directions for Burying Me 9
Discovery 12
Disquieting Figures 127
Distinguished College 130
Dobie Arrives 124
Dobie Signs Again 130
Doctor 11
Dr. Townsend Himself 84
Dr. Vinton 52
Dodd, Lee Wilson 151
Dog Around the Block 15
Doily Menace 45
Door 83
"Door," "The Professor," "My Friend the Poet (Deceased)," "The Washable House," and "The Man Out in Jersey" 148
Doormat 45
Dove's Nest 71
Down East with E. B. White 150
Downhill All the Way 123
Dream Children: A Reverie 44
Drifting Whither with E. B. White 152
Drill Schedule 125
Driving of the Rivet 15
Duncan Borg 50
Dunning, Philip 135
Dusk in Fierce Pajamas 66

E. B. W. 147
E. B. White 147, 148, 150
E. B. White: A Man of Letters 150
E. B. White: A Treasury of that Modest, Wise and Witty Master 158
E. B. White, "Farmer/Other" 149
E. B. White Forever 160
E. B. White ... Greatness in Miniature 163
E. B. White Letters Provide a Constant Delight 163
E. B. White: Notes and Comment by Author 149
E. B. White on the Exercycle 163
E. B. White Reader 7
E. B. White Recalls Cornell Years 149
E. B. White Surveys His World 154
E. B. White Takes on Xerox and Wins 150
E. B. White, That Fine Goldsmith in Words 156
E. B. White's Civilized Way of Saying Things 160
E. B. White's Tale of Swans and Children Delights & Instructs 161
E. Bagworm Wren 65
Ear Pictures 69
Earl Carroll's Vanities 133, 135
Earthbound Boy 21
Earthy, Humorous, Accessible 154
Eastern Standard 11
Editorial: The Vile Vendetta of the ... 124
Editorial: Whatever May Be the ... 124
Editors 36, 143
Editors of the New Yorker 32
Edman, Irwin 153, 154, 156, 158
Education Revolutionized? 131
Eeny Meeny Miny Mo 52
Egg Is All 122
Eight-Year-Olds Tangled in "Charlotte's Web" 148
Election 128
Electric Fences, Poets, Etc. 84
Elegant Slums 33
Elements of Style 6
"Elements of Style" in Revised Edition 159
Elevated 28
Eligibility 127
Ellege, Scott 149, 154
Elliott Sender 70
Elmer Gantry 133
Elmer Hostetter 43
Embryo Classic 128
Erlanger, Aline 133
Ernst, Morris L. 136

Essays of E. B. White 7
Essences 14
Ethics Club 131
Euller, Carol Nauth 158
Eustace Tilley 52, 78
Eva the Fifth 134
Eve of St. Francis 97
Even the horse was sick of the whole business 144
Evening on Ice 29
Ever Popular Am I, Mammoth, Wilt Resistant 24
Ever Upward 35
Everyday Is Saturday 5
Eviction 31
Excellence of Speech 130
Exchange Classes 126
Expectancy 11
Exploration 28
Extra Hour 131
Ex-Uncle 48
Ezra Cornell 130

F. A. O. 53
F. P. A. 143
Faculty Should Ratify 131
Faculty Tea Party 128
Faculty Wants to Know 130
Fad or a Fixture 125
Fadiman, Clifton 147, 153
Fair Defeat 128
Fair Judgment 127
Fair Play 66
Fairfax Vinton 47
Faith of a Writer: Remarks Upon Reveiving the 1971 National Medal for Literature 122
Fall Creek Natatorium 126
Family Which Dwelt Apart 81
Farewell, My Lovely 75
Farewell to Model T 5
Farmer's Week 131
Farming Under Water, etc. 82
Fashions in Dogs 20
Fatal Interview: A Volume of Love Sonnets 136
Fate of a System 126
Father Does His Best 16
Fay, Frank 135
Federalist at Three A. M. 108

Feet of the Mayor of Clay 24
Feld, Rose 154
Fenton, John H. 148
Ferguson, Otis 153, 154
Festival Chorus 125
Fifty-Two American Moods 81
Figure It Out 126
Figures 131
Fin de Saison--Palm Beach 67
Fire! 130
Firebug's Homecoming 144
Firefly 134
First Cornell President 124
First Freedom 136
First Night 17
First of All, Good Citizenship 125
First Person Singular 154
Fish Wing 41
Fisher, Emma 150
Five Little Lessons 129
Five O'Clock 12
Flocks We Watch by Night 84
Flying Colors 135
Flying Ever Ethiopian Mountain Ranges 20
Flying Over 41
Flying Slow 54
Foibles of 1840 128
Food for Thought 128
Football 127
Football and Psychology 129
Football Captain 128
Footlight Parade 135
For Future Historians 152
For Mutual Benefit 128
For Serena, Keeper of the Draw-Curtains 15
For They Teach Not Their Own Use 129
For Things That Are a Part of Me 11
For Your Information, Senator 82
Ford, George 134
Forward Glance O'er the Obituary Page 23
Fount 51
Four Miles Over Timber 59
Fox of Peapack 14
Fox of Peapack, and Other Poems 5
Frank Perry 142
Frank, Susan I. 149
Franklin Delano Roosevelt 143

Franks, Lucinda 150
Frascino, Edward 7
Fred on Space 119
Free 34
Free Concert 125
Free Speech and Bad Judgment 129
Freedman, Richard 164
Freedom Medal Honors Kennedy 149
Freshman Rules 126
Freshman Tax 126
Friendly 31
Frigidity in Men 46
Friml, Rudolph 134
From an Office 11
Front Page 133
Fuller, Edmund 160, 161, 163
Fuller, John Wesley 148
Funny Stands 125

G. S. Lobrano 143
G. W. Bridge 56
Gag 53
Gag Man Has a Horrid Dream 12
Gang War 134
Garter Motif 27
General Examination 130
General Survey of Early Summer in Town and Country 19
Gentlemen of the Press 134
Gershwin, George 134
Gershwin, Ira 134
Get Rid of New Jersey 33
Getting Along with Women 73
Getting Away 38
Getting It There 54
Getting Through the Day 27
Gil Borg 58
Gill, Brendan 150
Go Climb a More Meaningful Tree 148
Go Jump in the Sea Dept. 101
Goin' Home 134
Goings on in the Barnyard 123
Gold, Herbert 160
Good Fairy 134
Good Votes Lost 127
Goodwin, Polly 161
Governor Alfred E. Smith 127

Gramercy Park 13
Grant, Jane 149
Graph Showing Fluctuation in Relations Between France and the United States During Fiscal Good Will Period 33
Gray, Geraldine 158
Great Indoors 79
Greek Games 75
Green Hill Far Away 81
Green Thumb in a Mass of Clenched Fists 162
Grew, William A. 133
Growing Up in New Canaan 58
Guests at Cornell 125
Guide to the Pronunciation of Words in "Time" 75
Guns 133
Guth, Dorothy Lobrano 7
Gynt, Kaj. 133

H. L. Mencken Meets a Poet in the West Side Y.M.C.A. 75
H. W. Ross 143
Hagan, James 133
Hail Britannica Our Eye 14
Hail to Franklin D. Roosevelt 19
Hall, Donald 163
Hallowe'en Rush 128
Hammer 29
Hammerstein, Arthur 134
Harbach, Otto 134
Harbinger 28
Harbor Lady 38
Hardy Band 130
Hark! Hark! The Turncoats 57
Harper to Mifflin to Chance 17
Harriett 37
Harvard's System 128
Harvest of Half-Truths 16
Hasley, Louis 150
Hatton, Fanny 135
Hatton, Frederic 135
Have a Thought 125
Hawthorn Hill 20
He 36
He Understood Women 133
He was never more boring than when he was sleeping 144
Headlines 128
Heart Throbs 36
Hearths 130

Hecht, Ben 133
Heins, Paul 161
Helen 39
Helen E. Hopkinson 143
Hello 127
Henson, Harry 151
Hentoff, Margaret 162
Here Is New York 105
Here Is New York 6
Here Today 134
Hey Day Labor 27
Heyward, Donald 133
Heywood, Donald 135
Hicks, Granville 151, 159
Higgins, Judith 162
High School Oracle 124
Higher the Drier 129
Historic 32
Historical 45
Ho Hum, Newsbreaks from "The New Yorker" 5
Hoboken Nights 40
Hockey Again 130
Hodges, Elizabeth 158
Hogan, William 159, 160
Holidays Are Sad Days for People Who Don't Have Holidays 18
Hollis E. Dann 127
Hollywood and a Nervous Dog 83
Homer, Frank X. J. 163
Honor to Scholarship 124
Honorary Society Eligibility 125
Hoover Meeting 125
Hoover on the Job 131
Hopkins, Lee Bennet 150
Horniman, Roy 134
Horse Mart 31
Hotel Anthology 9
Hotspur the Swift 43
Hour of Letdown 110
How Big Is Cornell? 126
How Far to Go 131
How Many Students 126
How the Automobile Got into Bermuda 81
How to Be Elegant 32
How to Break a Rib 153
How to Drive the New Ford 35
How to Make a Cat Trap 50

How to Study Effectively 8
How to Tell a Major Poet from a Minor Poet 51
Howard, Janet 162
Howdy, King; Howdy, Queen 31
Howes, Raymond Floyd 138
Humanity and Humor 154
Humorist 153
Humorist with a Heart 159
Humors and Careers 147
Hunger 53
Hungry Scufflers 129
Huntsman, I'm in a Quarry 85
Husbands and Wives 22
Hyman, Stanley E. 154
Hymn to the Dark 19

I Accept with Widespread Pleasure 90
I Am Dying to Know What You Are Saying, Egypt 24
I Expect a Cow 89
I Paint What I See 17, 122
I Say to You, Cheerio 20
I Spy 23
I Take a Poll 86
I Want to Be Insured by Calvin Coolidge 14
Ice Pond 78
Ice Water 125
I'd Send my Son to Cornell
If You Say So 26
Imperial Airways 13
In a Deceased Doughnut Factory 8
In a Garden 9
In and Out of Books 148
In Central Park 91
In Charlie's Bar 122
In Gallipolis the Bells Are Tolling 20
In Praise of E. B. White, Realist 147
In Quest of E. B. White 150
In Re Gladness 9
In Re Life 44
<u>In Times Square</u> 134
Independent Organization 129
Independent Tea Dance 130
<u>Individualism, Old and New</u> 136
Ingersoll, Ralph 147
Inner-Spring Mattresses 21
Intercollegiate Vote 127

Interesting Discovery 33
Interim 40
Interpretation 44
Interview with a Sparrow 30
Interview with Daisy 52
Interview with Mr. E. B. White, Essayist 147
Intimations at Fifty-Eighth Street 12
Intimations--Not of Immortality 13
Inviting Disaster 132
Iron Man 18
Irtnog 73
Is a Train 19
Is Prose Dead? Not to E. B. White 163
Is Sex Necessary? or, Why You Feel the Way You Do 5
Is This the Time? 130
Isadora's Brother 47
It's a 'ome 42
It's About Time Department 56
It's Coming On 131
It's Spring, Spring in Pittsfield, Mass. 20

Jackson, J. H. 156, 158
Jackson, Joseph 134
Jacob Gould Sherman, Cornellian 124
James Hannon 142
James Thurber 143
Jiu-Jitsu 61
Job for the Council 131
John Ferguson 135
John Fitzgerald Kennedy 143
John Hoyle 127
John J. Carney 129
Johnson Returns 47
Joint Meetings 128
Joke in the Constitution 130
Jones, Roy Edwin 138
Journalism at Cornell 125
Journeys 10
Journey's Dead-End 62
Julius Ceasar 133
Jungle Flower 18
Jury Duty 9

Kallesser, Michael 133
Kanfer, Stefan 163

Kaufman, George S. 134
Kearney, Patrick 133
Keep the Title 131
Kellman, Amy 161
Key Men 54
Key of Life 56
Khrushchev and I 119
Kieran, Margaret Ford 157
Kight, Margie 158
King and His Ladye 20
King's English 126
Kiniery, Paul 157
Kinkead, Eugene 138
Kinkead, Katharine T. 157
Kirk, at Harvard, Asks Free Inquiry 148
Kiss Me 133
Kramer, Dale 148
Krutch, Joseph Wood 158
Kunitz, Stanley J. 147

Lack of Discipline 126
Lacrosse as a Game 125
Lacrosse Season 126
Lady Before Breakfast 72
Lady Is Cold 5
Lady of the Chorus Watches Dorothy Stone 27
Lamour Sells Bonds 89
Landslide 61
Last Day 17
Last Look Around 154
Last Minute Jam 131
Laughter, Not Immoderate 154
Laura Ingalls Wilder Acceptance, Address, June 30, 1970 122
Law of the Jungle 18
Law of the Land 127
Lawn Dance 11
Lawson, John Howard 135
Leacock's University 128
Leaderless Team 129
Lee Strout White 75
Let the Council Know 129
Letter (Delayed) from the North 120
Letter from the East 117, 118, 119, 122, 123
Letter from the North 119
Letter from the South 118

Letter from the West 119
Letter to the Editor 144
Letter to the Editor: The Age of Fear--Mr. White Thinks We Fell Over the Cat 144
Letter to the Editor: These Edgy Times--Mr. White Believes Us Needlessly Unkind 144
Letters of E. B. White 7
Letters We Never Finished Reading 43
Levy, Benn W. 134
Liberal in a Lounge Chair 81
Librarian Said It Was Bad for Children 121
Library Lion Speaks 11
Life Cycle of a Literary Genius 27
Life in the Barn Was Very Good 157
Life of Spice 19
Life Triumphant 91
Light That Failed 27
Light Verse 151
Lightest of the Arts 152
Likes and Dislikes 152
Lilly Turner 135
Lime, Dogs, etc. 86
Linder, Mark 135
Lindquist, Jennie D. 157
Line Forms in Front of Morrill 127
Lines 25
Lines for an Amaryllis Keeper 15
Lines in Anguish 28
Lines Long After Santayana 18
Listen, Baby 33
Listener's Guide to the Birds 25
Literary Business 67
Little Harmony 128
Little Lessons in Probation 126, 127
Little Man 27
Little Penn Game 128
Little Women 134
Lives and Times of Archy and Mehitabel 138
Lobstering and Freedom 84
Locke, Edward 135
Lombardy, Ltd. 133
Lonely Hearts 39
Looks Low, Is Low 103
Lopsided 29
Lots of Candidates 128
Love 16
Love Affair with America 88

Love Among the Foreign Offices 22
Love in a Garden 12
Love Letter to Manhattan 157
Lower Level 27
Lullaby for a City Baby 12
Lunch Hour 12
Lure of the Sea 128
Lynch, Frances 133

M. R. A. 84
MacArthur, Charles 133
McCord, David 152
McGowen, John 135
Mack, Willard 134
McPherson, William 162
Madam X 133
Magic 70
Make-Believe 34
Make Good the Trust 131
Makings of a Union 127
Malabar Farm 23, 137
Mall 18, 43
Mall Life 63
Maloney, Russell 148
Mammy India 36
Man I Saw 15
Man in 32 57
Man Out in Jersey 149
Man Who Changed in Appearance 80
Man Who Reclaimed His Head 134
Man Without a Title 128
Manhatters 133
Manuscript Club 26
Many Happy Returns 66
Marble from Steel 37
Marble-Top 11
Marquis, Don 138
Marvin, John R. 162
Mask and an Unveiling 163
Master of Sense and Sentences 152
Mate-of-the-Month Club 30
Mating Season 133
Matter of Opinion 127
M'Baby Loves Me 29
Meet Penn with Penn Tactics 130
Memo for an Unclaimed Pad 17

Memoirs of a Dramatic Critic 40
Memoirs of a Master 84
Memorandum for an Infant Boy 17
Meridian Seven 16
Message: To Be Dropped Inside Russia from a Gas Balloon 24
Mexican Suit 30
Meyer, Cord, Jr. 136
Middle Class 67
Middleton, George 134
Midsummer Night's Dream 133
Midwinter Madness 58
Military Department 125
Milk and Water 52
Millay, Edna St. Vincent 136
Miniature 41
Miracle of the Classroom 127
Miss Gulliver Travels 134
Misstep 25
Mr. Mackenzie 131
Mr. Maloney's Ginsberg 53
Mr. Volente 87
Mr. White Surveys the World 155
Mr. White's "Trumpet of the Swan" Is an Elegiac If One-Key Pastorale 161
Mitchell, Dobson L. 134
Mitgang, Herbert 150
Model Oh! 34
Modern Hiawatha 8
Modern Man of Walden 149
Molasses in January 78
Molnar, Ferenc 134
Money in the Bank Helps Not the [sic] 17
Money Lender 134
Monograph with Punch 151
Montparnasse 38
Moore, Anne Carroll 157
Morando, Estelle 135
"More Liberal" Plan 131
More Power to You! A Working Technique for Making the Most of Human Energy 136
Morehouse, Ward 134
Moritz, Charles 148
Morning of the Day They Did It 107
Morning Worship 51
Morningtime and Eveningtime 89
Morrill Hospitality 127

Motor Boat Show 62, 70
Motorless Flight 49
Mouse & Moujik 155
Mrs. Little's Second Son 155
Much Ado About Plenty 72
Muddy Stream 129
Muggeridge, Malcolm 163
Multitude of Topics Touched by a True Master of Style 160
Muscles on High 43
Muse and the Mug 22
Music Festival 126
Musical Clubs 131
Mutilated Cap 125
My Childhood Bends Beside Me 157
My Day 87
My Friend the Poet (Deceased) 148
My Little Cabin Monoplane 40
My Man 67
My Physical Handicap, Ha, Ha 80

Namesake 47
Natura in Urbe 13
Navigation 13
Near-Demise of Mrs. Coe 53
New Party 130
New Rushing Rules 125
New York Alumni 128
New York Child's Garden of Voices 10
New Yorker 147
Newer Art 131
News Outside the Door 65
Next Step 125
Next Year's Rushing 129
Nichols, Anne 133
Nick Bawlf 126
1931-- 134
1921's Chance 125
No Half Way Mark 130
No Hands 153
No Hat 28
No Matter What the Skirt Length Is, Every Prospect Pleases Me, Because I Am Vile 23
No Place to Hide 137
No Reply Yet, or Undank Ist der Welt-Lohn 28
Noise for Dartmouth 128
Nona 135

Non-Fraternity 129
Non-Negotiable 127
Noontime of an Advertising Man 106
Nordell, Roderick 148, 160, 163
Nordstrom, Ursula 150
Norris, Charles G. 136
North, Clyde 134
Northern 39
Northwestern 128
Not Big But Great 130
Note 107
Notes and Comment 27-123
Notes for a Ludwig 42
Notes for a New Whirl Symphony 17
Notes from a Desk Calendar 12
Now That I'm Organized 34
Nugatory 12
Nulton, Lucy 148

Obituary 58
Observation 19
Observation Train 126
O'Connell, Shaun 163
Of Beauty and Consternation 163
Of Thee I Sing 134
Of Things That Are 14
Off for England 129
O.K. to Go Ahead, or How Police Horses Are Trained 42
Ol' Man North River 13
Ol' Man Satan 135
Old Algiers 49
Old Boys Cavort 126
Old Clocks 40
Old Coon Dog Scolds a Pup 117
Old Open Busses 80
Old Roads of Long Island 64
Old Yell 125
Omnibus 144
On Listening Ears 126
Once More to the Lake 87
One Flag for One World 156
One Man's Meat 82-91
One Man's Meat 6
One Man's Meat by E. B. White 154
1000 Reasons, All Good 153
One Year Old 29

Ontario 14
Onward and Upward with the Arts 67, 69, 71, 74, 75, 81
Open Discussion 124
Open Letter to My Burgler 28
Open Letter to the Department of Correction 38
Open-Letters Department 78
Open Reply to Mrs. Mendelson 41
Openings 34
Oppenheimer, George S. 133, 134
Orange Juice 21
Origins 17
Other 4, 999 125
Other Side of the Case 50
Our Captious Readers 10
Our Contentious Readers 85
Our Disillusioned Readers 50
Our Foreign Policy 137
Our Impressionable Readers 99
Our little son must never know 143
Our Major Minor Sport 131
Our Own Controversy 32
Our Postponed Easter 132
Our Tardy Readers 69
Our Windswept Correspondents: The Eye of Edna 116
Ourselves and Others 129
Out of Town: Snow Train 70
Outposts 54
Overall for Girls and Men 125
Owl in the Attic 138

P. B. Publico 79
Padlocks of 1927 133
Page Mr. Moakley 129
Palace Thoughts 24
Pale Hands, Form 1040, Search for a Sleigh, etc. 85
Paradise Lost: Book IV 9
Paramore, Edward E., Jr. 134
Parker, Dorothy 136
Parolers 131
Passing Bad Paper 131
Passing of Alpheus W. Halliday 24
Passing of the Wet One 127
Passing Present 134
Passionate Passenger to His Love 20
Past and Present 128
Pastoral 46

Pasture Management 23
Peace or Anarchy 136
Pearl Harbor Investigation 22
Pember, Clifford 134
Penn Game 125
Percentage of Women 126
Percy Field Today 125
Percy Field Will Be Ready 126
Peripatetic Reviewer 156, 157, 159, 161
Personal Column 139, 140
Personal Ships 55
Peskiness and Peace 21
Petit Dejeuner 27
Petition for Journalism 125
Phenomenon of the Cork Smeller 127
Philip Wedge 42
Philips, Murray 133
Pierce, Noel 135
Pigeon, Sing Cuccu 20
Pink Hats 26
Pitkin, Walter B. 136
Plan 13
Plan for Peace 137
Pledge in Good Faith 127
Plimpton, George A. 149
Poco Agitato 27
Poet, or the Growth of a Literary Figure 14
Poets Are Being Watched 36
Point of View 126
Pointers for Statesman or Skeptic 156
Points of My Compass: Letters from the East, the West, the North, the South 6
"Points of My Compass: Letters from the East, the West, the North, the South," by E. B. White 160
Pooch Palace 77
Poor Pole 128
Poore, Charles 156
Portrait of a Poet at the Dome 11
Potter's Field 37
Poughkeepsie at Poughkeepsie 126
Pour le Sport 62
Practical Farmer 86
Preaching Humorist 87
Predatory 29
Prelim Period 129
Preposterous Parables 80, 81, 83, 102
Presenting the Belmont Bar 49

President for Cornell 126
Press Service 8
Pretty Good Place 130
Probation 126
Problems of Rushing 131
Production 126
Profession of a New Yorker 158
Professor 33
Professor Stagg's Appointment 129
Professor's Job 126
Profiles: Little Monarch 54
Program 12
Promenade 130
Prospectus 125
Psalm of David Smith 16
Psychology of the Bull Session, or, The Professor in the Home 129
Public Force of a Private Man 163
Public Speaking 126
Pullmanism 36
Pulse-Quickening 75

Quarter of a Million 126
Question, More or Less Direct 17
Quiet Wit of E. B. White 164
Quo Vadimus? 49
Quo Vadimus? or, The Case for the Bicycle 6

R. F. Tweedle D. 81
Rabbi and Judge 35
Raison, Milton 134
Rang Tang 133
Raphael, John 133
Ratio of Colleges 129
Raymont, Henry 149
Reader's Choice 160
"Reader's Digest" Discovers the Bible 79
Reader's Report 138
Reading Mrs. Lindbergh 86
Real Estate 11
Receiving Line 27
Red Blooded Reformers 130
Red Cow Is Dead 22
Relations 134
Remarks 150

Renting the Leviathan 27
Reporter at Large 41, 48, 54, 58, 59, 65, 83, 97
Reporter at Sea 69
Repudiation 129
Respectability of the Drag 127
Rest Room No. 2 41
Retort Transcendental 88
Return of the Teams 124
Returning 10
Revived Art 124
Rhyme for a Reasonable Lady 14
Rhideout, Ransom 134
Right Balance 127
Right of Privacy 144
Ring Lardner 142
Ringing Steel 28
Ringside 134
Rising Mercury 125
Ritual for a Restaurant 10
Road by a River 14
Romance of the Publishing Game 42
Roosevelts: Just Roosevelts 60
Rose, Carl 144
Rosenfeld, Isaac 156
Round and Round 43
Royal 29
Rubbing Elbows 31
Rude 44
Ruins 11
Rules for Good Writing 159
Runners 46
Rush 127
Rushing 126
Rusty Pilots 125
Ryskin, Morrie 134

S. Finny 45, 134
Safekeeping of ... Enchantment 160
St. John, Ervine 135
St. Nicholas League 69
Sampson, Edward C. 150
Saturday Night 127
Saul Wright 133
Saving the Free Press 150
Schoenfeld, Bernard C. 135
School of Journalism at Cornell 124

Schott, Webster 160
Schuman and the League 127
Schwartz, Arthur 135
Scriba, Jay 150
Scrub 128
Sea and the Wind That Blows 120
Sea Beacon 41
Second Call to Arms 87
Second Comin' 134
Second Term Initiation 125
Second Tree from the Corner 101
Second Tree from the Corner 6
Seed, a Novel of Birth Control 136
Seeing Gloria Plain 46
Seeing Shelley Plain 42
Seeing So Many Fezzes ... 114
Seeing Things 36
Semi-Annual Mercy 126
Senator Cartwright 129
Send-Off: Frannie J. Reed 142
Senior Banquet 125
Seniors Doing Lessons 131
Sense and Style 158
September Rain 11
Sequoia, How Oya? 19
Seriously Un-Serious 162
Serpent in the Gorge 125
Seven Steps to Heaven 119
Sevenfold Pooh 86
Sex Racket 43
Shady Lady 135
Shaw-Terry Letters 16
She married me for my muscular system 144
Sheed, Wilfred 162
Shenandoah Road 10
Shenker, Israel 149
Sherman, Beatrice 152
Sherwood, Robert E. 158
Shoot the Works 134
Shooting Star 135
Shoppers 22
Shrine 32
Sifton, Clair 134
Sifton, Paul 134
Silence of the Gears 18
Simon, Max 133
Simpler for Cabinet Members 17

Simpler Rushing 131
Sinking of the Scharnhorst 21
Sinkside Reverie 23
Sitting Song 13
Sixth Avenue El 82
Sixty to Nothing 127
Size of the Vote 131
Sleight of Hand 41
Slow Freights 49
Small Thanks to You 81
Smaridge, Norah 149
Smilin' Through 164
Smith, Paul Gerard 133
Snakes 32
Snakes' Supper 48
Snappy 33
Snood and Its Relation to Me 21
s'nospmohT 55
So I Ups to Morgan 17
Social Life at Williams 131
Soglow, O. 5
Soliloquy at Times Square 13
Something for Seniors 131
Song for Before Breakfast 13
Song for the Delegates 16
Song from an X-Ray Table 17
Song of the Middle Years 21
Song of the Queen Bee 22
Song to be Disregarded 13
Song Writer 133
Sonnet 14
Soprano 12
Sound Doctrine 129
Soviet Teacher 130
Spade-Calling 52
Spain in Fifty-Ninth Street 19
Span 43
Spare Rooms 128
Speaking of Books 147, 153
Speaking of Counterweights 82
Special Luncheon 68
Spectorsky, A. C. 138
Spells 71
Spewack, Bella 135
Spewack, Samuel 135
Spider, Egg, and Microcosm: Three Men and Three Worlds of Science 138

Spinach 144
Spirit of St. Christopher 13
Spoken Word 127
Sporting Chance 126
Sporting Proposition 127
Spring Football 125
Spring, Stove, etc. 87
Springtime Crossroad Episode in Four-Time 24
Springtime for Henry 134
Square Thing 127
Squire Cuthbert 67
Stafford, Jean 161, 162
Stand Down, Ye Pusillanimous Rascals 23
Start Running 126
State of the States 96
Statement of the Foreign Policy of One Citizen of the United States 18
Steinoff, William R. 148
Stenersen, Stanley G. 163
Step Forward 26
Step Toward a Goal 129
Sterling Finny Advertisements 143, 144
Still Waters 85
Stone Unturned 124
Stork Is Dead 135
Straight Up 71
Stratagem for Retirement 118
Straw Vote 125
Street Corner on a Lesser Doomsday 17
Street of the Dead 70
Strike at the Leisure Plant 81
Strunk, William, Jr. 6
Stuart Little 6
Stuart Little: or, New York Through the Eyes of a Mouse 155
Stuart, Wilbur, Charlotte: A Tale of Tales 150
Student Judiciary 125
Study of the Clinical "We" 63
Subtreasury of American Humor 6
Subway People 10
Subway Trouble Explained 37
Success Story 135
Suggested Telegrams 31
Sugrue, Thomas 157
Suits for Jimmy 40
Sun, 1920-1921 124

Sunday 13
Sunday Baseball 126
Sunday Morning Radio 83
Sunset Gun 136
Superficiality 129
Supervising the College Man 126
Supremacy of Uruguay 65
Survival Through Adaptation 25
Sutherland, Zena 161
Swell Steerage 27
Swing Low, Sweet Upswing 61
Syracuse--Cornell 126
Syracuse Tragedy 132

Table for One 25
Take a Letter to Thoreau 84
Take a Vote 125
Talk About Girls 133
Talk of the Town and Country: E. B. White 150
Tangible Magic 157
Tattle Tales 135
Taylor, Ethel 134
Tea Taster 38
Teaching Trinity 138
Tell 'Em the Truth 129
Tempestuous Teapot 129
Tennis 24
Tennis Association 127
Terse Verse 71
Testing the Prophets 88
Thankless Guest Exposes Lyric Host 19
That Goes for You, Siegfried 20
Then and Now 65
There Is No Marion Davies 34
There's a Tower in the Sky 11
These Precious Days 142
They Come with Joyous Song 83
They giggled when he stirred the soup with his finger 143
They Have Never Kept a Secret from Us Yet 15
They Shall Not Pass 127
They wondered why the caddy walked away 144
They're Off 128
Things That Bother Me 30
This Is a Prayer Before I Sleep 14
This is capital fun for me! 143

This Is the Girl I'm Going to Marry 46
Thomas, A. E. 134, 135
Thomas Mott Osborne 125
Thoreau, Henry David 136, 138
Thoreau on a Roof Garden 152
Those Locker Coupons 124
Thoughts on Where to Live 19
Thoughts--While Minding a Sleeping Infant Belonging to Someone Else 31
Thoughts While Skating 240 Laps at the Ice Club 35
Thoughts While Sowing Five Pounds of Domestic Rye Grass Seed at 40 Cents the Pound 24
301 Mott 38
Three Hundred Years Ago 129
Three Owl's Notebook 157
<u>Thunder Over Mexico</u> 135
Thurber, James 5, 138, 147
Tidbits & Pieces 158
Tifft 31
Tilley the Toiler: A Profile of the New Yorker Magazine 148
Timid Nautilus 16
To a Hot Water Bottle Named Jonathan 13
To a Lady Across the Way 13
To a Lady Who Was Once a Freshman 14
To a Perfumed Lady at the Concert 16
To a Perhaps Unavoidably Late Rose 15
To an Outstanding Woman 19
To Bust or Not to Bust 124
To Do It Well and Not for Gain 129
To F. P. A., Who Finds Kansas Scenery Dull 9
To Hotspur, Departed 8
To Morvich, Winner 8
To My Dog, Leaving Me 8
To Serena on a September Day 15
To the Memory of Hotspur, a Model "T" 12
To the Princess on Her Birthday 23
To the Woolworth Building 8
Today I Should 87
Toller, Ernest 134
Tombes, Andrew 133
Tombs Are Best 32
Too Soon Forgotten 128
Topics: An Act of Intellect to Turn the Year 121
Topics: Dear Mr. ... 121
Topics: Our New Countryman at the U. N. 121
Tourist-Camps 77
Town Report--A Plan for America 84

Traction Corporation 127
Traction Service 129
Trade Winds 157
Trade Winds: Comment 112
Trade Winds: Reply 144
Trader Horn 36
Tragedy of the Unimpassioned 128
Training for Officers 129
Translations from the Calvinese 15
Traveler in Reality 148
Traveler's Song 15
Travers, P. L. 157
Treasures Upon Earth 37
Trees 78
Trees for Radio City 83
Trees of Winter 15
Trial Blue Sunday 129
Trilling, Diana 154
Triplets 135
Triumphant Defeat 130
Trivia 53
True Dog Story 26
Trumpet of the Swan 7
Tubes 11
Tuning in Through Georgia 9
Tunney's Little Man 39
Turtle Bay Diary 101
Twentieth Century Gets Through 14
Two Conclusions 130
Two Identical Parties 129
Two Kinds of Athletics 127
Two Letters, Both Open 109
Two Meals Today 130
Typewriter Man 148

Ubiquitous Canine 124
Uncle Tom's Cabin 135
Under a Steamer Rug 22
Under the Lindens 76
Underground Resistances 18
Undeserved Bricks 128
Unger, Gladys 135
Untrodden Ways 125
Unwinding 25
Updike, John 150, 161, 163
Upside Down 28

Urban New-Yorker 154
Urgency of an Agency 53
U.S. Department of State 137

V-23 62
Van Druten, John 134
Van Gelder, Robert 147
Van Horne, Geneva P. 158
Van Sickle, Raymond 135
Variant 14
Variety Show 134
Vermin 22
Verse Sweetens Toil 18
Vestigial Organs 44
Village Gardens 76
Village Revisited 22
Visit 54
Visiting Teams 128
Visitors to the Pond 114
Voices 51
Vote on the Honor System 131

Walden 136, 138
Walden--1954 116
Walker, Stanley 153, 160
Walter Hampden 129
Walter Tithridge, M.D. 85
Walton, Eda Lou 151
Waltz Time 135
Wanted--A Junior Week System 130
War Being Over 44
War-Time Diary 84
Was Lifted by Ears as Boy, No Harm Done 120
Washable House 148
Washing Up 57
Watson, Mark S. 155
Watt, William W. 6, 7
Way of Living 34
Wayward Press: Scoops and Denials 45
We 31
We Will Not Report 131
Weales, Gerald 149, 162
Weatherby, W. J. 149
Weber, L. Lawrence 135
Webster, Harvey Curtis 158

Weekend with the Angels 93
Weeks, Edward 153, 154, 156, 157, 159, 161
Welcome Home 130
Well, in the last chapter ... 101
Well-Shod Boy 21
Welty, Eudora 157, 164
West Farm Jottings 43
What Do Our Hearts Treasure? 121
What Every Adult Should Know 35
What Goes On 124
What Hitler Has Done 87
What Is a Class? 125
What Is at Stake? 131
What Is Cheerleading? 126
What, Ma, No Jam? 28
What of the Age? 130
What Should Children Tell Parents? 47
What the Constitution Provides 131
What to Wear 126
What Will the Faculty Do? 130
Whee-e! 43
When Ladies Meet 135
When the Team Goes 128
When to Eat 125
Where Are the Diabolos? 47
Where Do the New Eras Go? 40
Where Is Tennis 127
Where Welcome Waits 9
White, Katharine S. 6, 155
White Enjoys Relaxed Climate with Picturesque View of Bay 149
White House Callers 86
White of the Rueful Countenance 163
White Papers: First Class Mail 162
White's Letter to Ellsworth American 123
White's Letter to Xerox 123
White's Letters: The Lofty with the Mundane 163
Who Buys 127
Who Shall Decide 131
Why a Bonus? 125
Why Albert Ferncroft Is a Bitter Man 29
Why I Like New York 26
Why Minor Sport? 125
Why You Should Go 125
Wilbur, Crane 133
Wild Flag: Editorials from the New Yorker on Federal World Government and Other Matters 6

Williams, Clarence 133
Williams, Garth 6
Willis, Katherine Tappert 155
Wilson, Hazel 161
Window Ledge in the Atom Age 22
Wings of Orville 55
Winter into Spring 30
Winter Sports 129
Wintle, Justin 150
With Asterisks 84
With Camera and Codkerel 35
With War Declared 87
Wolcott Gibbs 143
Woman in Bronze 133
Wonder 56
Wonder and Wackiness of Man 158
Words 12
World Girdling 20
World Government and Peace: Selected Notes and Comment 6
World Is Heard From 125
World of E. B. White 160
Worm Turning 33
Writer as Private Man 148
Writer at Large 162
Wulff, Derick 133
Wyath, E. V. R. 154

X in Examination 126

Yachts 30
Yardley, Jonathan 163
Yates, Norris W. 149
You are a saintly woman--and that about covers it! 143
You Can't Resettle Me! A Defense of New York by a Stubborn Inhabitant 77
Young Advertising Man, After a Hard Day at the Office, Writes to the Girl He Loves 9
Yours of the Ult., Ours of the Inst. 36
Yule Neurosis Sifted in Report 116

Zephyr 67
Zoo Things 37